A Standing Miracle

Pivotal Events *that* Sparked a Revolution *and* Led to America's Independence

DENNIS PARKER

AUTHOR OF *Jefferson's Masterpiece*

Copyright 2018
© Dennis Parker
All Rights Reserved
Printed in the United States of America

ISBN: 978-0-692-17674-0

Cover and Book Design by Beverly E. Parker

JeffersonsMasterpiece.com

Acknowledgements

The true authors of *A Standing Miracle* are the American colonists.
It was through their determination, persistence, courage
and strong will, during a troubling and uncertain period of 20 years,
that led to the creation of a free and independent United States of America.

My sincere thanks to Jill Via, Denise Parker and Beverly E. Parker
for their valuable contributions to this book.

I wish to acknowledge that *A Standing Miracle* could not
have been written without the scholarly research and written word
of so many people over the past two-plus centuries.

> The original spelling, punctuation and capitalization
> in the eighteenth century writings
> that appear in this book have been retained.

Table of Contents

"Little Short of A Standing Miracle" 1
Introduction 2

Prelude to War

1763 4
1764 7
1765 9
1766 11
1767 13
1768 14
1769 16
1770 17
1771 18
1772 19
1773 20
1774 22

American Revolution

1775 24
1776 38
1777 53
1778 59
1779 60
1780 61
1781 64
1782 69

Peace and Freedom

1783 70
Treaty of Paris 71
Bibliography 72
Image Credits 72

"Little Short of a Standing Miracle"

In his Farewell Orders to the Continental Army on November 2, 1783,
General George Washington shared his impressions
on the stunning accomplishments of America's Continental Army.

*"The disadvantageous circumstances on our part,
under which the war was undertaken, can never be forgotten.
The singular interpositions of Providence
in our feeble condition were such,
as could scarcely escape the attention
of the most unobserving; while the unparalleled perseverance
of the Armies of the United States,
through almost every possible suffering and discouragement
for the space of eight long years,
was a little short of a standing miracle."*

FROM PEAC

A Standing Miracle tells the amazing story of America's struggle for independence.

E TO WAR

Independence Not Easily Nor Quickly Achieved

The American colonists lived in peaceful harmony under British rule in the years prior to the American Revolution. King George III and Parliament had little interest in the growing colonies during the late 17th and early 18th centuries.

During that time the colonists enjoyed tranquil peace, freedom and prosperity. They experienced limited self-government and were able to tax themselves with little interference from the British monarchy. The colonists were proud to be part of the British Empire and to call themselves Englishmen.

In 1696, they experienced new freedom when Parliament passed the Salutary Act that relaxed the enforcement of regulations and laws that had been imposed on the 13 colonies. As a result, the Americans had more flexibility to govern themselves, as well as the economic and political freedom to achieve greater prosperity.

However, the Salutary Act did not prevent Parliament from passing laws that restricted the manufacture of wool, hats, pig iron and iron bars; imposed heavy taxes on molasses, rum and sugar imported from non-British colonies; and regulated overseas trade that protected the profits of English merchants while severely limiting the ability of Americans to trade with non-British companies.

British authorities reversed the Salutary Act's policies after the French and Indian War.

King George III's first act was to issue the Proclamation of 1763 that prohibited American settlers from establishing homes in territory west of the Appalachian Mountains.

His Proclamation was followed by a long list of offensive taxes, tariffs, restrictions, rules and penalties. Each new tax and restriction prompted the colonists to begin thinking about independence from the British government.

A Standing Miracle tells the incredible story of how the American colonists moved from being *British subjects* to becoming *citizens of the United States of America.* The book chronicles 20 years of struggles and sacrifices the Americans endured to obtain freedom from British domination. Comprehensive-yearly timelines and short narratives provide insights into the events and activities that produced a revolution and the Declaration of Independence. The story is enhanced by a variety of diverse topics that highlight the personal side of this amazing miracle. Another feature is the host of reproductions of original documents and color images that help to visualize this multifaceted historical event.

A Standing Miracle is the timeless story of the brave men and women who achieved the impossible – the creation of the Unites States of America.

American Colonies Before the Revolutionary War

1763

- **FEBRUARY 10 - BRITISH ACTION:** The French and Indian War ended with Great Britain winning control of Canada and the American Midwest.
- **OCTOBER 7 - BRITISH ACTION:** King George III issued the Proclamation of 1763 that forbid colonists from settling on land west of the Appalachian Mountains and required those already living there to move east.

Long Struggle for Independence Began

The seeds of conflict between the American colonies and Great Britain started months after the French and Indian War ended in 1763.

The French and Indian War was fought because of an ongoing dispute between Great Britain and France about who controlled the land between the British and French territories in northern North American. Before the war started in 1754, Great Britain controlled the territory occupied by the 13 colonies east of the Appalachian Mountains. France controlled the large area west of the Appalachians that extended from Louisiana to Canada.

The disputed territory centered around France's expansion into the Ohio River Valley which conflicted with Britain's claims. The lucrative fur trade and access to the Mississippi River added to the tensions between the two countries.

After years of fighting, the war ended with Great Britain the victor. The terms of the 1763 Treaty of Paris awarded Great Britain the vast French territory east of the Mississippi River and north of Spanish Florida. King George III's government was left with an enormous debt, uncertainty about how to govern the new territory, and how to keep peace with the Indians.

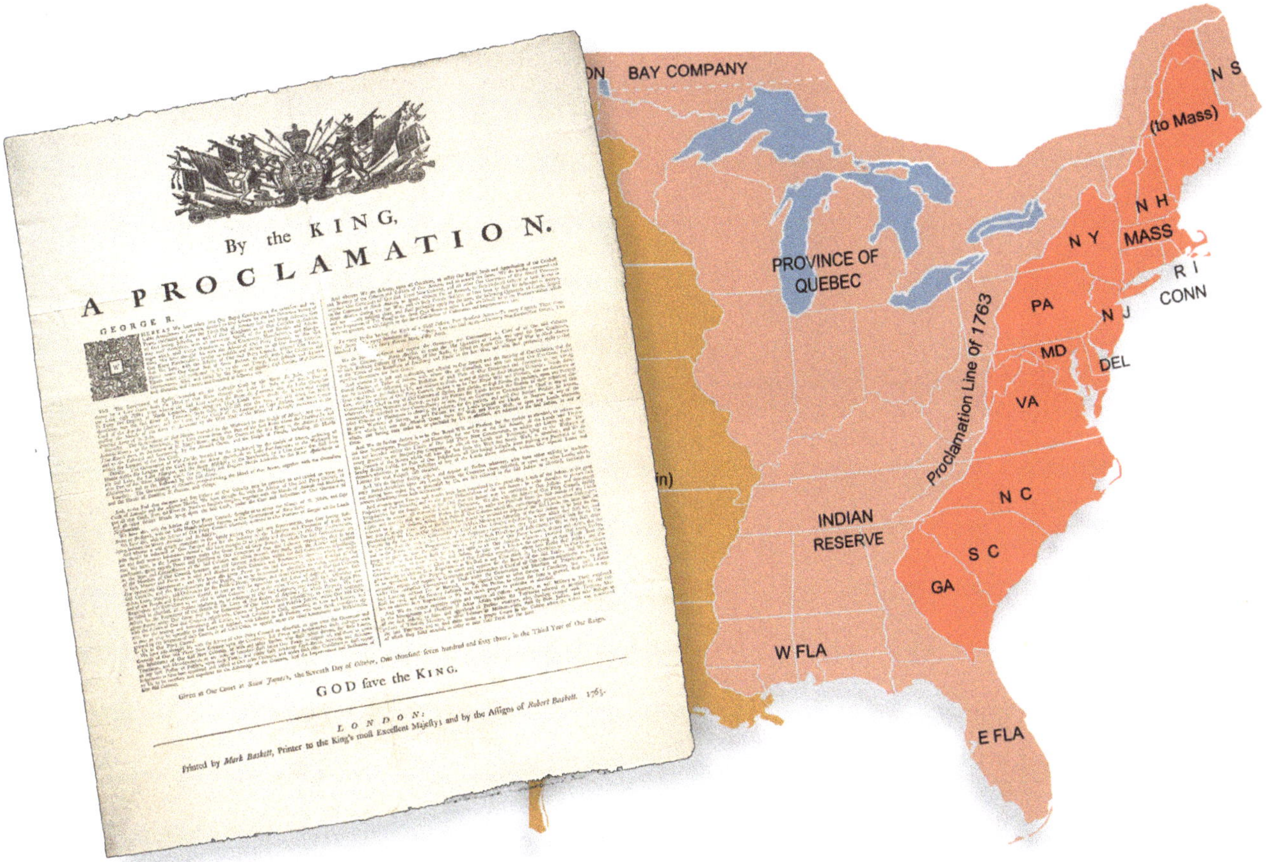

King George III Closed Frontier to Colonials

King George III issued the Royal Proclamation of 1763 on October 7 following Great Britain's victory in the French and Indian War. Because of the victory, Great Britain acquired a vast, rich territory in North America. The Proclamation closed the frontier to colonial expansion west of the Appalachian Mountains, including the Ohio, Tennessee and Florida territories.

The King's original intent was to reserve the land for the Indian tribes that fought alongside British troops during the war. He wanted to avoid future conflicts between American settlers and the Indians.

Americans saw the Proclamation as an infringement on their rights. This greatly angered his American subjects, but it did not stop them from continuing to move west. Wagon loads of pioneering families, led by men like Daniel Boone, traveled across the mountains to settle on the rich, fertile lands beyond the Appalachian Mountains.

The Proclamation of 1763 was the first in a long list of British policies, taxes and actions that would lead to the American Revolution and the Declaration of Independence.

The Colonies

When the Colonies Were Founded:
1607 – Virginia
1620 – Massachusetts
1626 – New York
1633 – Maryland
1636 – Rhode Island
1636 – Connecticut
1638 – Delaware
1638 – New Hampshire
1653 – North Carolina
1663 – South Carolina
1664 – New Jersey
1682 – Pennsylvania
1732 – Georgia

Three Types of British Colonies
• **ROYAL COLONIES** were governed directly by the British government through a royal governor appointed by the Crown: New Hampshire, New York, New Jersey, Virginia, North Carolina, South Carolina and Georgia.
• **CHARTER COLONIES** were granted to business owners who established the laws based on English laws: Connecticut, Massachusetts, Rhode Island and Virginia.
• **PROPRIETARY COLONIES** were owned by one person or a family: Delaware, Maryland and Pennsylvania. The proprietor had full governing rights.

The colonies were established to provide raw materials that would benefit the British economy and help grow the British Empire. They were allowed to exercise limited self-government and to collect taxes, under the supervision of royal government officials.

Who Were the Patriots?
• Patriots wanted the American colonies to be independent from the British monarchy.
• Patriots believed the British government was treating them unjustly and unfairly.
• Patriots wanted to govern themselves in their own independent country.

Who Were the Loyalists?
• Loyalists wanted to remain part of the British empire and enjoy the security and benefits of being British citizens.
• Loyalists believed their lives would be better if they lived under British rule instead of a patriot government.
• Loyalists were afraid that American independence would end or jeopardize their business or family connections in England.

Communications, Currency & Taxes, Taxes, Taxes!

1764

- **APRIL 5** - **BRITISH ACTION:** The British Parliament passed the Sugar Act to offset the war debt from the French and Indian War, and to help pay the expenses of running the colonies and governing the newly acquired territories.
- **MAY 28** - **AMERICAN ACTION:** At a Boston town meeting, James Otis raised the issue of "taxation without representation" – a phrase that he reportedly coined. He also urged a united response of opposition to the laws imposed by the King and Parliament.
- **JULY** - **AMERICAN ACTION:** James Otis published *The Rights of the British Colonies Asserted and Proved.* He denied Parliament's authority to tax the colonies and favored American representation in Parliament. His paper argued that English liberties provided protection from internal taxation without representation in Parliament and provided safeguards against threats to life, liberty and property.
- **AUGUST** - **AMERICAN ACTION:** Boston merchants agreed to boycott British luxury goods.
- **SEPTEMBER 1** - **BRITISH ACTION:** The Currency Act approved by Parliament prohibited the colonists from issuing legal tender paper money. The goal was to destabilize the American economy. **AMERICAN RESPONSE:** Colonists became united in their opposition to the Currency Act.

James Otis, *The Rights of the British Colonies Asserted and Proved*

James Otis argued that Americans had the same rights and privileges as all "fellow subjects in Great Britain." His pamphlet was a protest to the Sugar Act. He became a leader in America's fight against King George III's tyrannical rule.

He wrote: "Every British subject born on the continent of America . . . is by the law of God and nature, by the common law, and by acts of parliament, entitled to all the natural, essential, inherent and inseparable rights of our fellow subjects in Great Britain. . . . The end of government being the good of mankind, points out its great duties: It is above all things to provide for the security, the quiet, and happy enjoyment of life, liberty and property."

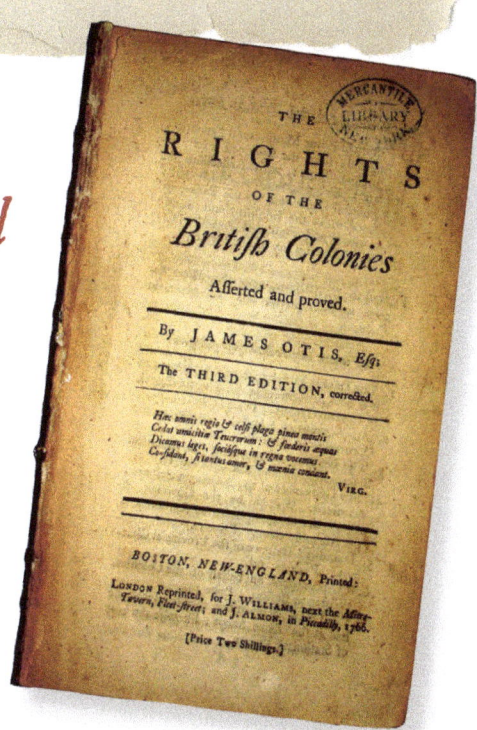

Third Edition printed in 1766.

British Took Control of the Colonial Economy

Parliament passed the Currency Act on September 1, 1764, which prohibited the issue of new paper money and the reissue of existing paper money throughout the 13 colonies.

Because of the mercantile system that the colonies worked under, there was always a shortage of hard currency (silver and gold) to conduct trade and commerce. Silver and gold coins could only be obtained through British regulated trade. That left the colonies with only one alternative, to print their own money. However, this posed a major problem. The value of colonial bills was always changing because the money was not backed by anything of standard value, like gold or silver. This forced many merchants, citizens and British businessmen to refuse to accept the almost worthless paper money.

The Currency Act did not benefit the colonies; it only benefited British business interests.

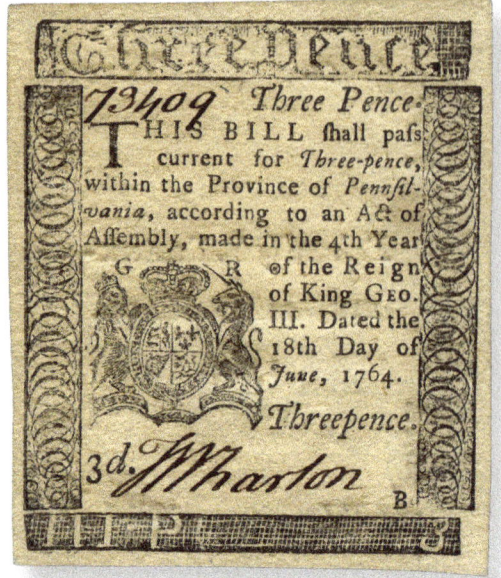

Three Pence Note
The Three Pence note was issued in the Province of Pennsylvania. It was printed by Benjamin Franklin and David Hall.

The Currency Act approved by Parliament prohibited the colonists from issuing legal tender paper money.

Sugar Act Attempted to Stop Colonial Smuggling

Parliament enacted the Sugar Tax on April 5, 1764. It was an extension of the 1733 Molasses Act. The overall goal was to raise revenue from the American colonists to defray the military costs of protecting the colonies, and to repay the huge debt left from the French and Indian War.

Parliament wanted to discourage colonial merchants from smuggling molasses and other goods into the colonies. Merchants did not pay taxes on smuggled items.

The Sugar Act reduced the tax on molasses and sugar to encourage colonial merchants to buy molasses from British colonies instead of smuggling it from French and Spanish colonies. The Act also included provisions that strengthened the enforcement of smuggling laws.

Parliament Increased Pressure

1765

- **MARCH 22** - BRITISH ACTION: Parliament passed the Stamp Act to offset the high costs of British military operation in America. AMERICAN RESPONSE: Colonists quickly united in opposition to the Stamp Act taxes.
- **MARCH 24** - BRITISH ACTION: Parliament's Quartering Act required colonists to lodge British troops in their homes and provide them with food.
- **MAY 30** - AMERICAN ACTION: The Virginia House of Burgesses adopted resolutions entitled the Virginia Resolves, which were written and presented by Patrick Henry.
- **JULY** - AMERICAN ACTION: The Sons of Liberty, an underground organization opposed to the Stamp Act, was formed in Boston.
- **OCTOBER 7 to 25** - AMERICAN ACTION: The Stamp Act Congress convened in New York City with 27 men representing 9 colonies. Congress adopted The Declaration of Rights and Grievances that included 13 resolutions which were sent to King George III and Parliament. BRITISH ACTION: The King rejected the petition because he claimed it was submitted by an unconstitutional assembly.
- **NOVEMBER 1** - AMERICAN ACTION: Most business and legal transactions in the colonies were terminated when the Stamp Act went into effect. Nearly all the colonists refused to use the stamps.
- **DECEMBER 13** - BRITISH ACTION: British Major General Thomas Gage, commander of English military forces in America, asked the New York Assembly to force the colonists to comply with the Quartering Act.
- **DECEMBER** - AMERICAN ACTION: The boycott of English imports spread as more than 200 Boston merchants joined the movement.

First Direct Tax on the Colonists

The Stamp Act that passed Parliament on March 22, 1765, was the first internal tax directly levied on the American colonists. It taxed all legal documents, newspapers, almanacs, pamphlets, broadsides, ship's papers, licenses, dice and playing cards.

The purpose of the tax was to help pay for British soldiers to defend and protect the American frontier – the area beyond the Appalachian Mountains.

Prior to the Stamp Act, colonial taxes were to regulate commerce, not to raise money. American colonists were afraid the Stamp Act had paved the way for similar taxes without first getting the consent of the colonial legislatures or through direct American representation in Parliament.

Patrick Henry protested the Stamp Act.

The Stamp Act was repealed in 1766. However, Parliament enacted the Declaratory Act at the same time, which reaffirmed Parliament's authority to pass any legislation it deemed necessary for the colonies.

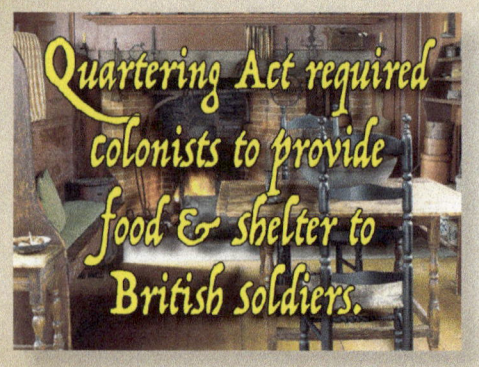

Parliament passed the Quartering Act on March 24, 1765. The Americans did not want British soldiers living and eating in their homes. But, there was nothing they could do about it.

Parliament's Taxing Authority Questioned

"Caesar had his Brutus, Charles the First his Cromwell; and George the Third may profit by their example. If this be treason, make the most of it." ~ Patrick Henry's speech to the Virginia House of Burgesses on the Virginia Resolves.

Patrick Henry introduced a series of resolutions to the Virginia House of Burgesses on May 29, 1765. His resolutions were in response to the Stamp Act that taxed every piece of printed paper the American colonists used.

Henry was a new member and had only served for nine days. He was an outspoken opponent of British policies.

The Virginia Resolves disputed Parliament's right to tax American colonists and stated that colonial assemblies possessed the exclusive power to tax their citizens.

By the end of 1765, eight other colonies had adopted similar resolves.

Stamp Act
Colonies United to Fight Stamps

The Stamp Act Congress was the first time representatives from the colonies had ever met to work on common problems. Twenty-seven delegates from nine colonies met from October 7-25, 1765, in New York City's Federal Hall. New Hampshire, Virginia, North Carolina and Georgia did not send representatives.

In addition to adopting a unified protest against the Stamp Act, the delegates issued a Declaration of Rights and Grievances that stated:
- As British subjects, they had the same rights as British subjects living in Britain.
- Only the colonial assemblies had a right to tax the colonies.
- They were free from taxes except those they had given their consent.
- They had the right to trial by jury.

The Declaration of Rights and Grievances was sent to King George III and Parliament along with a request that Parliament repeal the Stamp Act, the Sugar Act and the Currency Act.

Sons of Liberty
Secret Organization Paved the Way

The Sons of Liberty was a secret organization established to undermine British rule in colonial America. Its origins are unclear, but the earliest historical references are found in Boston and New York in 1765. Popular belief is that the organization was started by Samuel Adams and John Hancock after news of the Stamp Act became known. Their motto was, "No taxation without representation."

Membership consisted of males from all walks of colonial society. By 1766, Sons of Liberty chapters were in every colony.

Their public demonstrations, fear and intimidation tactics, and the stockpiling of arms and ammunition, helped to undermine British authority. They provided the spirit and enthusiasm, and were the foot soldiers of a movement that paved the way for America's independence.

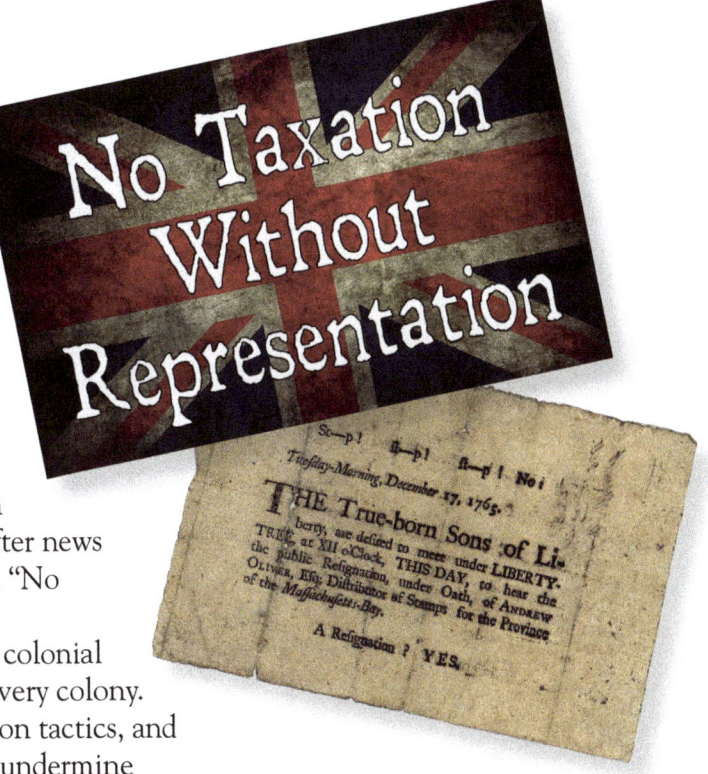

Newspaper notice announcing a Sons of Liberty meeting.

Resistance Continues

1766

- **JANUARY - AMERICAN ACTION:** The New York Assembly refused to comply with General Gage's request to enforce the Quartering Act.
- **MARCH 18 - BRITISH ACTION:** Parliament passed the Declaratory Act that asserted that the British government had total power to legislate any laws governing the American colonies.
- **MARCH 18 - BRITISH ACTION:** Parliament repealed the Stamp Act.
- **APRIL - AMERICAN ACTION:** Celebrations took place throughout the colonies with the news that the Stamp Act had been repealed. The repeal caused a relaxation of the American boycott of English goods.
- **AUGUST - AMERICAN ACTION:** Violence broke out in New York between British soldiers and armed colonists. The violence erupted because many New Yorkers refused to comply with the Quartering Act.
- **DECEMBER 13 - BRITISH ACTION:** Major General Thomas Gage suspended the New York Assembly for refusing to comply with the Quartering Act. This was done to make an example to the other colonies.

Declaratory Act: Parliament Tightened Controls

Parliament passed the Declaratory Act on March 18, 1766, as a reaction to America's rejection of the Stamp Act. Parliament and the King did not expect this law to be controversial.

Parliament also repealed the Stamp Act at the same time. The Declaratory Act made it crystal clear that:

• Parliament had full power and authority to make laws binding the American colonies "in all cases whatsoever," including the right to tax.

• The American colonies were under the authority of the British crown, and any colonial laws or regulations that denied or questioned Parliament's power and authority were null and void.

The colonists were outraged by this new law. They did not believe the British government had the right to control their lives and property, especially a governing body that was thousands of miles away and knew nothing about their lives, economy or customs.

"I rejoice that America has resisted," stated William Pitt, a member of the British Parliament, when he learned that Americans had vigorously opposed the Declaratory Act.

> Parliament wanted the Americans to know that they had full control over the colonies, not their local governments.

Parliament Imposed Townshend Acts

1767

- **JUNE 15** - BRITISH ACTION: Parliament adopted the New York Restraining Act - the first of the Townshend Acts - that forbade the New York Assembly and the governor from making laws until they agreed to comply with the Quartering Act.
- **JUNE 29** - BRITISH ACTION: Parliament passed three additional Townshend Acts: the Revenue Act that imposed tariffs on glass, lead, painters colors, tea and paper imported to America; the Indemnity Act that reduced taxes on East India Company tea; and the Commissioners of Customs Act that authorized tougher enforcement of custom regulations.
- **OCTOBER** - AMERICAN ACTION: Town meeting in Boston renewed its call for a boycott of British luxury items.

Townshend Acts

The British government passed five laws in 1767 and 1768, known as the Townshend Acts, that were designed to raise revenue from the colonists and enforce the crown's authority on the American colonies.

The NEW YORK RESTRAINING ACT (June 15, 1767) forbade the New York Assembly and the Governor of New York from passing any new bills until they agreed to comply with the Quartering Act of 1765, which required them to provide housing, food and supplies to British troops in the colony.

The REVENUE ACT (June 29, 1767) set new import taxes on painters colors, paper, lead, glass and tea. The revenues were to maintain British troops in America and to pay the salaries of royal officials who were appointed to work in America. It gave customs officials broad authority to enforce the taxes and punish smugglers.

The INDEMNITY ACT (June 29, 1767) reduced taxes on East India Company tea, which make the tea cost less than the tea colonial merchants were smuggling from Holland. This allowed merchants to import British tea at cheaper prices and resell it at prices lower than the Holland tea.

The COMMISSIONERS OF CUSTOMS ACT (June 29, 1767) authorized tougher enforcement of custom regulations that included hiring new customs officers and tax collectors. It created a new Customs Board for the North American colonies headquartered in Boston. New offices were authorized to be opened in other colonial ports.

The VICE ADMIRALTY COURT ACT (July 6, 1768) created new Admiralty Courts to prosecute colonial smugglers. The act gave Royal Naval Courts jurisdiction over all matters concerning customs violations and smuggling, rather than colonial courts. Three new Royal Admiralty Courts were established in Boston, Philadelphia and Charleston. The verdicts of the Admiralty Courts were to be decided by the judge, not by a jury. In addition to their salaries, judges received a monetary award when smugglers were found guilty.

On April 12, 1770, Parliament voted to repeal the Townshend Acts, except for the tax on tea.

East India Company Insignia

Circular Letter, Protests & Boycotts

1768

- **FEBRUARY 11 - AMERICAN ACTION:** Sam Adams wrote a Circular Letter that opposed taxation without representation and called for colonists to unite against the British government.
- **APRIL 22 - BRITISH ACTION:** England's Secretary of State for the Colonies, Lord Hillsborough, ordered colonial governors to stop their assemblies from endorsing Adams' Circular Letter. Hillsborough also ordered the Governor of Massachusetts to dissolve the General Court if the Massachusetts Assembly refused to revoke the letter.
- **APRIL - AMERICAN ACTION:** The assemblies of New Hampshire, Connecticut and New Jersey endorsed Sam Adams' Circular Letter.
- **MAY 17 - BRITISH ACTION:** A British warship armed with 50 cannons sailed into Boston Harbor and aimed its cannons toward Boston.
- **JUNE 17 - BRITISH ACTION:** Massachusetts Governor Francis Bernard dissolved the General Court after the Massachusetts Assembly defied his order to revoke Adams' Circular Letter.
- **JULY 6 - BRITISH ACTION:** Parliament passed the final Townshend Act. It created new Admiralty Courts to prosecute colonial smugglers; gave Royal Naval Courts jurisdiction over customs violations and smuggling; and established three Royal Admiralty Courts.
- **AUGUST - AMERICAN ACTION:** Boston and New York merchants agreed to boycott British goods until the Townshend Acts were repealed.
- **SEPTEMBER - BRITISH ACTION:** British warships sailed into Boston Harbor with two regiments of Redcoats and began to occupy Boston. The purpose of the military occupation was to enforce the Townshend Acts and to suppress the actions of local patriots.
- **SEPTEMBER - AMERICAN ACTION:** At a town meeting, Boston residents were urged to arm themselves in response to the military occupation.

Circular Letter Angered British Government

In February 1768, the Massachusetts House of Representatives sent a letter to the colonies encouraging unified opposition to the Townshend Acts. Sam Adams argued that the acts were unconstitutional because Massachusetts was not represented in Parliament. He also declared that England's Parliament could not violate the British Constitution or the natural rights of colonists.

King George III responded by issuing a warning to the colonial legislatures to treat the Circular Letter with contempt and threatened to dissolve any legislative body that supported it.

Father of the American Revolution

Sam Adams is known as the "Father of the American Revolution" and "Father of American Independence."

He earned these titles because of the hundreds of opinion articles he wrote for Boston newspapers, and for the protests he led against what he believed to be a British plot to destroy constitutional liberty. His writings helped build public opinion in favor of a separation from Great Britain. He led the way with his ardent defense of colonial Americans' rights to take actions against the British monarchy.

Sam Adams was a brilliant strategist and skillful organizer who developed the concept of non-violent citizen resistance. His actions led to protests against the Sugar Act, Stamp Act and other laws affecting the colonies. In addition, he played a leading role in the creation of the Sons of Liberty, the Committees of Correspondence, the Tea Party and the Continental Congress.

Through his dedication and hard work, the Boston rabble rouser played a leading role in the creation of the United States of America.

"The natural liberty of man is to be free from any superior power on Earth, and not to be under the will or legislative authority of man, but only to have the law of nature for his rule." - Sam Adams

British Occupation

The seven year British occupation of Boston began in late September 1768 when 4,000 British troops landed in Boston Harbor.

After widespread protests against the Townshend Acts, Massachusetts Governor Francis Bernard requested that British troops be stationed in Boston. This convinced British officials that they needed troops to maintain order and enforce Parliament's laws in Boston.

This bold British move, plus, the Sugar Act, Currency Act, Quartering Act and Townshend Acts as well as the *Romney*, a British man-of-war docked in the Boston Harbor with its 50 cannons aimed toward Boston, greatly increased the outrage of Boston citizens.

The occupation caused large numbers of Boston patriots to move to the countryside. Patriot sympathizers were largely in control of the villages outside of Boston. Living conditions inside the city became unbearable with severe shortages of food, firewood and everyday commodities. Vacant homes, shops and warehouses were used to lodge British officers and troops, or they would be torn apart for firewood or anything that could be burned in fireplaces. Boston was not a good place to live during the occupation.

American Resistance Increased
1769

- **MARCH** - AMERICAN ACTION: Philadelphia merchants joined the boycott of British goods.
- **MAY 17** - BRITISH ACTION: In retaliation to the House of Burgesses adopting the Virginia Resolves, Royal Governor Baron de Botetourt dissolved the House of Burgesses. AMERICAN ACTION: Members of the House of Burgesses immediately moved to the Apollo Room in Williamsburg's Raleigh Tavern and resumed their meeting.
- **OCTOBER** - AMERICAN ACTION: Merchants in New Jersey, Rhode Island and North Carolina joined the boycott of British goods.

Governor Dissolved House of Burgesses

Virginia Royal Governor Baron de Botetourt dissolved the Virginia House of Burgesses on May 17, 1769. He was unhappy that the House had protested so strongly against the Townshend Acts. The burgesses were not disturbed by his action. The 89 members adjourned and calmly walked down the street to the Raleigh Tavern where they reconvened their meeting in the Apollo Room.

Raleigh Tavern in Willamsburg, Virginia, was a center of activity in the colonial era. Washington and Jefferson were patrons. Today the restoration is so complete one can almost hear the strains of music, the click of dice and the clank of pewter tankards.

While at the Raleigh Tavern, among other business, they adopted a Non-Importation Agreement and created a standing Committee of Correspondence. The Non-Importation Agreement was a voluntary accord to stop the purchase of goods from British merchants until the royal government changed its policies.

Patriot merchants in New Jersey, Rhode Island and North Carolina joined the boycott.

The Governor reconvened the House of Burgesses later that year in November.

"... the Battle of King Street..."
1770

- **JANUARY 17 - AMERICAN ACTION:** Violence erupted in New York City when citizens tried to stop British soldiers from cutting down the liberty pole.
- **MARCH 5 - BRITISH ACTION:** The Boston Massacre took place after a group of Boston citizens taunted British soldiers guarding the Customs House.
- **APRIL 12 - BRITISH ACTION:** Parliament repealed the Townshend Acts. All duties on imports into the colonies were eliminated, except for tea. Parliament also refused to renew the 1765 Quartering Act.

Boston Massacre

"On that night the formation of American independence was laid… Not the battle of Lexington or Bunker Hill, not the surrender of Burgoyne or Cornwallis were more important events in American history than the battle of King Street on March 5th 1770." - John Adams

British soldiers killed three Boston citizens on the night of March 5, 1770, including Crispus Attucks, a free man of African and Native American descent. Two died later from gun shot wounds and six more had nonlethal wounds. This event became known as the Boston Massacre.

An anti-British mood had been growing in Boston since 4,000 troops occupied the city in September of 1768. The troops were sent to enforce the Townshend Acts that were unpopular in Boston and throughout the colonies. Clashes between soldiers and citizens had become a normal occurrence.

The violence began as an argument between a British sentry and Boston residents outside the Custom House where British officials collected import duties. The argument escalated as more colonists gathered.

Captain Thomas Preston, the officer in charge, sent six privates and a corporal to support the sentry. They lined up facing the crowd and were ordered to load their muskets and fix their bayonets. The captain tried to get the growing crowd to leave. But the appearance and actions of the troops provoked the unarmed citizens even more. Within seconds, an object was thrown that struck a soldier. This was followed by a volley of shots from the soldiers. When the smoke cleared, dead and wounded Bostonians were lying between the soldiers and the crowd.

Captain Preston and his men were tried for murder. John Adams and Josiah Quincy agreed to defend the soldiers. Adams said he defended them to demonstrate the impartiality of the colonial judicial system. Preston and six of his men were acquitted; two others were found guilty of manslaughter, punished and discharged.

As word spread about the Boston Massacre, American support for independence took a significant leap.

Backcountry Settlers Rebelled

1771

• MAY 16 - AMERICAN ACTION: The Battle of Alamance was fought between North Carolina backcountry settlers - called Regulators - and militia loyal to Governor William Tryon.

Governor's Militia Took Fight to Backcountry Settlers

The Battle of Alamance on May 16, 1771, took place six years after the Regulator Movement started in Piedmont North Carolina. The rebellion of backcountry settlers - called Regulators - was a protest against royal authority, excessive taxes and dishonest sheriffs.

Since the Piedmont settlers were primarily farmers who raised crops for their families and bartered for goods and services, they had little or no money for taxes or government fees. They became debtors to their local governments.

Hostility between the Regulators and government officials came to a critical point in 1771. North Carolina Governor William Tryon's council advised him to call out the militia to find the Regulators and convince them to stop their rebellion.

In May, Governor Tryon marched 1,000 militiamen to Alamance Creek. He discovered a large number of Regulators camped about six miles away. On May 15, a band of Regulators captured two of the governor's militiamen which angered the governor. He sent a messenger to tell the Regulators, estimated to be around 2,000, that they should disband.

The Regulators answered with this message: "Fire and be damned!" The governor gave the order on May 16, and the rebellion was crushed after a two-hour battle.

The North Carolina militia suffered nine killed and 61 wounded. The Regulators' losses are unknown but believed to be much greater. Fifteen Regulators were taken prisoner and seven were hanged.

The Regulator movement is an example of how rebellion was growing throughout the colonies.

The rebellion of backcountry settlers, called Regulators, was a protest against royal authority, excessive taxes and dishonest sheriffs.

A Tea Act... Again

1772

- **MAY 10 - BRITISH ACTION:** Parliament approved a Tea Act that granted a monopoly to the East India Company to import tea into the American colonies.
- **JUNE 9 - AMERICAN ACTION:** The British customs schooner, the *Gaspée*, ran aground off Rhode Island in the Narragansett Bay. Citizens of Providence attacked and burned the ship.
- **NOVEMBER 2 - AMERICAN ACTION:** Sam Adams called a Boston town meeting. The citizens appointed a 21-member Committee of Correspondence that would share news with other towns.
- **NOVEMBER 20 - AMERICAN ACTION:** Sam Adams wrote the Rights of the Colonists, in which he listed and described the natural rights that American colonists should possess.

Gaspée Affair Helped Ignite Independence

On June 9, 1772, eight boatloads of Sons of Liberty men from Rhode Island looted and destroyed the revenue cutter *Gaspée* by fire. The ship had run aground chasing an American smuggling vessel. This action was not the first time Rhode Island patriots had attacked and destroyed British ships. In 1764, the *HMS St. John* was attacked and in 1769 the *HMS Liberty* was destroyed by fire.

Due to Great Britain's massive debt after the French and Indian War, Parliament decided to exert more control over the colonies that included new taxes and fees. One of their goals was to stop American smuggling. The Sons of Liberty responded to Parliament's tougher stand by carrying out acts of civil disobedience throughout the colonies.

British officials tried to bring the *Gaspée* raiding party to justice, but they were never punished.

The *Gaspée* affair was one of the early events that helped ignite the spark for American independence.

Colonists Stirred Into Action

1773

- **MARCH 12** - **AMERICAN ACTION:** The Virginia House of Burgesses appointed an 11 member Committee of Correspondence. Within a few months committees had been appointed in New Hampshire, Rhode Island, Connecticut and South Carolina.
- **MAY 10** - **BRITISH ACTION:** The Tea Act took effect on this date. It maintained the three-pence per pound tax on tea imported into the colonies. The Act also authorized the East India Company to ship half a million pounds of tea to its colonial tea agents.
- **OCTOBER 16** - **AMERICAN ACTION:** A mass meeting was held in Philadelphia to oppose the tea tax and the East India Company monopoly. A citizen-appointed committee met with the British tea agents and convinced them to resign.
- **NOVEMBER** - **AMERICAN ACTION:** A town meeting was held in Boston to endorse the actions taken by Philadelphia residents in October. Bostonians tried to get their British tea agents to resign, but failed.
- **NOVEMBER 28** - **BRITISH ACTION:** Three ships - the *Dartmouth*, *Eleanor* and *Beaver* - loaded with 342 chests of English tea sailed into Boston Harbor and anchored.
- **NOVEMBER 29 to 30** - **AMERICAN ACTION:** Two mass meetings were held in Boston on what to do about the three tea ships. They decided to send the tea on the *Dartmouth* back to England without paying the import duties. **BRITISH ACTION:** Massachusetts Royal Governor Hutchinson ordered harbor officials not to let the ship sail until the tea taxes were paid.
- **DECEMBER 16** - **AMERICAN ACTION:** About 8,000 Bostonians gathered to hear Sam Adams report that Royal Governor Hutchinson had repeated his earlier command not to allow the *Dartmouth* to leave until the taxes were paid. That night, the Boston Tea Party took place when colonial activists disguised as Mohawk Indians boarded the ships and dumped all 342 chests of tea into the harbor.

This notice from the *"Chairman of the Committee for Tarring and Feathering"* in Boston denounced the tea consignees as *"traitors to their country."*

Sons of Liberty Dumped the Tea

On December 16, 1773, about 60 members of the Boston Sons of Liberty, disguised as Mohawk Indians, boarded three British tea ships and dumped 342 chests (46 tons) of tea into the Boston Harbor. It took nearly three hours to complete the task.

The midnight raid was a protest against Parliament's passage of the 1773 Tea Act. Which upset the colonists, not only because of the tax, but also because a single company – the British East India Tea Company – would control all the tea imported into the colonies.

Parliament had granted a monopoly to the British East India Tea Company to sell tea at prices lower than Dutch smugglers had been selling to colonial merchants.

The arrival of the *Dartmouth*, *Eleanor* and *Beaver* caused an uproar among Boston citizens. The crisis came to a head when about 8,000 residents loudly protested on the wharf where the ships were docked.

A mass meeting was held later at the Old South Meeting House and demanded that the ships be sent back to England without paying the duty. Samuel Adams led a group to try to persuade Governor Thomas Hutchinson to release the ships. Adams reported back that Hutchinson had refused. As a result, a large crowd marched to the harbor about midnight and watched the disguised patriots throw the tea overboard.

> The arrival of three tea ships – the *Dartmouth*, the *Eleanor* and the *Beaver* – caused an uproar among Boston citizens.

Parliament Adopted Coercive Acts

1774

- **MARCH 31 to JUNE 22** - **BRITISH ACTION:** Parliament passed a series of acts known as the Coercive Acts (called Intolerable Acts in America) in response to the rebellion in Massachusetts.
- **MAY 12** - **AMERICAN ACTION:** In response to the Boston Port Act of the Coercive Acts, Boston citizens held a town meeting and called for a boycott of British imports.
- **MAY 13** - **BRITISH ACTION:** British General Thomas Gage, the new commander of British forces in the colonies, arrived in Boston. He placed Massachusetts under military rule and became Massachusetts' military governor.
- **MAY 17 to 23** - **AMERICAN ACTION:** Colonists in Providence, New York and Philadelphia called for an intercolonial congress to combat the Coercive Acts.
- **SEPTEMBER 1** - **BRITISH ACTION:** Military Governor General Thomas Gage seized the Massachusetts arsenal of weapons stored at Charlestown.
- **SEPTEMBER 5 to OCTOBER 26** - **AMERICAN ACTION:** The First Continental Congress met in Philadelphia with 56 delegates from every colony, except Georgia.
- **SEPTEMBER 17** - **AMERICAN ACTION:** Congress declared its opposition to the Coercive Acts, saying they are "not to be obeyed" and called for the formation of local militias.
- **OCTOBER 14** - **AMERICAN ACTION:** Congress adopted the Declaration and Resolves that expressed opposition to the Coercive Acts, the Quebec Act and other measures that undermined American colonial self-rule. The document asserted the rights of the colonists, including the rights to "life, liberty and property."
- **OCTOBER 20** - **AMERICAN ACTION:** Congress adopted the Continental Association that called for a boycott of English goods by all citizens and merchants; an embargo on the export of American products to Great Britain; and a termination of the slave trade.

"The die is now cast; the colonies must either submit or triumph… we must not retreat."

– King George III
Letter to Lord North, 1774

Coercive Acts Provided Ammunition

In reaction to the Boston Tea Party, Parliament enacted the Coercive Acts. The five acts were intended to punish the Bostonians for the Tea Party, for "unlawful" actions against British authority, and to restore order.

• MARCH 31 - The Boston Port Act closed the Boston Port until the East India Tea Company was reimbursed for the tea destroyed during the Tea Party.

• MAY 20 - The Massachusetts Government Act suspended the Massachusetts Charter of 1691; instituted a military government; forbade town meetings without approval; and made the governor's council a crown appointed body.

• MAY 20 - The Administration of Justice Act provided protection for British officials charged with crimes while on duty.

• JUNE 2 - The Quartering Act required each colony to provide housing, food and basic needs for British soldiers in private homes and uninhabited buildings.

• JUNE 22 - The Quebec Act reestablished Quebec's borders and granted it land in the Ohio Country; established a framework of government; restored French civil law; and granted freedom of religion to Roman Catholics.

The Coercive Acts provided ammunition for the growing unrest in the colonies and an increased desire for independence.

Delegates From 12 Colonies Met in Philadelphia

The first meeting of representatives from 12 of the 13 colonies was held on September 5, 1774, in Philadelphia at Carpenters' Hall. Fifty-six delegates attended the First Continental Congress. Georgia did not send representatives. The delegates met to provide a unified response to Parliament's passage of the Coercive Acts, which they believed were an infringement on the rights of all American colonists.

During its seven-week session, Congress issued a Declaration of Rights that affirmed America's loyalty to the British Crown, but protested the Coercive Acts and disputed Parliament's right to tax the colonies. It also passed the Articles of Association that called for the colonies not to import British goods beginning on December 1, 1774.

The Continental Congress assumed the role of coordinator for America's resistance against the King and Parliament's rule; provided liaison with Great Britain; and sought military and financial assistance from foreign governments.

An April Morning in Lexington and Concord

1775

- **FEBRUARY 9 - BRITISH ACTION:** Parliament declared Massachusetts to be in a state of rebellion.
- **MARCH 30 - BRITISH ACTION:** King George III endorsed the New England Restraining Act that required all New England colonies to trade exclusively with England, and banned fishing in the North Atlantic.
- **APRIL 14 - BRITISH ACTION:** Military Governor General Thomas Gage received orders to enforce the Coercive Acts and to suppress "open rebellion" among Massachusetts's citizens by all necessary force.
- **APRIL 18 - BRITISH ACTION:** Military Governor General Thomas Gage ordered 700 British soldiers to march to Concord and Lexington, Massachusetts, to destroy the patriot weapons depot.
- **APRIL 19 to MARCH 17 - AMERICAN ACTION:** The siege of Boston began after Lexington and Concord when militiamen from all over New England encircled Boston.
- **APRIL 23 - AMERICAN ACTION:** In response to the fighting at Lexington and Concord, the Massachusetts Provincial Congress ordered 13,600 soldiers to march to Boston to join the siege.

The War Started in Two Small Villages

The first shots fired between the American militia and the British Redcoats took place on April 19, 1775, in Lexington and Concord, Massachusetts.

British Major General Thomas Gage ordered Lieutenant Colonel Francis Smith to march 700 Redcoats to Concord to destroy muskets and pistols, power and musket balls, and cannons reportedly stored there by the patriots. They left Boston early on the morning of April 19. They would march through Lexington on their way to Concord.

Paul Revere and other riders warned the citizens that night about the approaching Redcoats. In the predawn hours, beating drums and peeling bells summoned 38 men and boys to the Lexington Green to join their commander Captain John Parker. They lined up and nervously waited for the British soldiers to come.

"Stand your ground, don't fire unless fired upon, but if they mean to have a war, let it begin here."
- Captain John Parker, Lexington Minuteman

The Redcoats marched into Lexington around 5 a.m. History does not record who fired the first shots *heard round the world*, but suddenly several Americans fell to the ground. The minutemen returned fire and soon began to retreat to avoid the heavy barrage of musket balls flying rapidly towards them. When the shooting stopped, eight minutemen had been killed and nine wounded.

The Redcoats searched the village but did not find any arms or munitions to destroy because it had been hidden. They also had been ordered to arrest Sam Adams and John Hancock, who had been meeting with other patriots. They could not be found.

Lieutenant Colonel Smith then marched his troops to Concord. An immediate search was ordered, but they only found three disabled cannons and several gun carriages that they burned. The patriots had been notified earlier by Dr. Samuel Prescott so they hid their arms and munitions.

A small battle took place on the North Bridge between the minutemen and a detachment of Redcoats. An exchange of gun fire took place, but since the British were vastly outnumbered, they retreated.

Around noon, Lieutenant Colonel Smith ordered his troops to begin the march back to Boston. He was not aware that word of the fighting had spread throughout the area and colonial militias were converging along Boston Road. As the Redcoats marched, minutemen fired at them from behind trees, fences and stonewalls.

Smith and his men were pleased that reinforcements were waiting in Lexington, but they had little effect. By the end of the day, British casualties totaled 73 killed and 173 wounded, with 50 Americans killed and 39 wounded.

Eyewitnesses Explained What They Saw

Artists Visited Lexington and Concord to Make Battle Scene Engravings

Weeks after the Battle of Lexington and Concord, Amos Doolittle, a young Connecticut engraver, visited the battlefields with a desire to recreate the scenes. He returned later with his friend, Ralph Earl, a portraitist. Doolittle interviewed the eyewitnesses to let them explain what they saw on that fateful day. Earl made sketches of the scenery, homes and buildings.

Earl used his sketches to paint the battlefield scenes. He filled in the troop positions and battle details with the information Doolittle had collected from the eyewitnesses. Doolittle assisted Earl by posing as local minutemen and Redcoats by holding a musket in his hand.

Back in his New Haven shop, Doolittle transferred Earl's color drawings onto copper plates for printing. They produced four scenes from the April 19 battles. On December 13, the printed sets were ready to sale. Each print contained the phrase, "neatly engraved on copper from the original paintings taken on the spot."

First-Hand Details Inspired Battle Engravings by Amos Doolittle, 1775

These are the only known contemporary portrayals of a Revolutionary War battle.

> "In Lexington the enemy set fire to Deacon Joseph Loring's house and barn, Mrs. Mullikin's house and shop, and Mr. Joshua Bond's house and shop, which were all consumed. They pillaged almost every house they passed by, breaking and destroying doors, windows, (looking) glasses, etc., and carrying off clothing and other valuable effects."
> - *Salem Gazette*, April 25, 1775

- **MAY 10 - AMERICAN ACTION:** American forces led by Ethan Allen and Benedict Arnold captured Fort Ticonderoga in New York. The captured military equipment and cannons were moved to Boston and used during the Boston siege.
- **MAY 10 - AMERICAN ACTION:** The Second Continental Congress convened in Philadelphia with John Hancock elected as president.
- **JUNE 14 - AMERICAN ACTION:** Congress established the Continental Army.
- **JUNE 15 - AMERICAN ACTION:** Congress unanimously voted to appoint George Washington to the post of Commander-in-Chief of the new Continental Army.
- **JUNE 17 - BRITISH ACTION:** The first major battle between British and American troops took place at the Battle of Bunker Hill.

2nd Continental Congress...
Oversaw the War and Declared Independence

The Second Continental Congress convened in Philadelphia's Pennsylvania State House on May 10, 1775, six months after the First Continental Congress adjourned.

As with the First Congress, the Second Continental Congress brought representatives from all 13 colonies together to lead a united resistance against the taxes, abuses and military threats of the British government. They were meeting right after the battles at Lexington and Concord, so the decision was still unclear as to what should be done.

Their major responsibilities were to unify and prepare the colonies for revolution; manage and finance the war; and encourage the colonies to contribute men, supplies and money. Congress's major achievements were to declare the colonies free and independent states, and the adoption of the Declaration of Independence.

This is the actual ground floor Assembly Room in the Pennsylvania State House where the Second Continental Congress met and made decisions that still affect our lives today. The delegates from each colony sat together at the green covered tables. President John Hancock presided from the raised table in the background. Congressional secretary, Charles Thomson, worked at the table near the door. (The Pennsylvania State House, now known as Independence Hall, is open to the public.)

Washington Took Command of Ragtag Army

General George Washington often stopped and talked with citizens as he journeyed to take command of the new Continental Army.

The Second Continental Congress unanimously appointed George Washington on June 15, 1775, as Commander-in-Chief of the new Continental Army. John Adams made the nomination.

At the time of his appointment Washington told Congress that he did not want to receive a salary. His only request was that his expenses be paid when the war ended.

Congress commissioned him with the rank of Commanding General. He had never commanded a large army in the field. His only prior military experience was during the French and Indian War, when he held the rank of major in the Virginia militia.

The new general took command on July 3, in Cambridge, Massachusetts, where thousands of militiamen from all over New England kept the British Army corralled inside Boston. The siege prevented the British army from leaving the city.

"This day I declare with the utmost sincerity, I do not think myself equal to the Command I am honoured with."

—Washington's Address to the Continental Congress after being appointed Commander-in-Chief

Bunker Hill, Massachusetts
Americans Lost First Battle Against Redcoats

Two months after the siege of Lexington and Concord, the first major battle took place on June 17, 1775, at Bunker Hill across from Boston.

In early June, British General Thomas Gage ordered General William Howe to occupy Bunker Hill. When the colonists learned about Gage's plan on the evening of June 16, American Colonel William Prescott led more than 1,000 troops to Bunker Hill to fortify the site. When they arrived they decided to fortify Breed's Hill instead. The officers thought Breed's Hill was a better site to defend against a British attack.

During the night, the Americans built a network of defensive earth breastworks, wood fences and stone walls.

At first light British commanders were surprised when they saw what the Americans had accomplished overnight. General Gage ordered General William Howe to attack with a force of 2,200 men.

> Everything was clearly visible to the many spectators crowded on hills, rooftops and steeples... including Abigail Adams and her young son, John Quincy, who cried at the flames and the "thunders" of British cannons.

When the British attack up the hill began, the Americans were ordered to hold their fire until the British were within 50 feet. A British officer described the scene: "Our Light Infantry were served up in companies and were devoured by musket fire." The British retreated on the first and second attacks. However, by this time the Americans were running low on ammunition. On the third attack the British succeeded. Most of the Americans were able to withdraw.

The British took control of Breed's Hill at a high cost of 268 killed and 828 wounded. The American casualties included 115 killed and 305 wounded.

- **JULY 3 - AMERICAN ACTION:** General George Washington took command of 17,000 militiamen stationed around Boston which became the Continental Army.
- **JULY 5 - AMERICAN ACTION:** The Second Continental Congress adopted the Olive Branch Petition that was addressed to King George III. It expressed hope for a reconciliation with Britain.
- **JULY 6 - AMERICAN ACTION:** The Second Continental Congress issued a Declaration on the Causes and Necessity of Taking Up Arms that provided reasons for fighting the British.
- **AUGUST - BRITISH ACTION:** King George III refused to look at the Olive Branch Petition and instead issued a proclamation that declared the American colonies to be in "open and avowed rebellion."

Olive Branch Petition
Congress Made One Last Appeal for Peace

The Second Continental Congress sent the Olive Branch Petition to King George III on July 5, 1775. Written by John Dickinson of Pennsylvania, the Petition was the last attempt by Congress to seek reconciliation with the British government. The delegates hoped their direct appeal to the King would avoid war.

The King refused to read the petition. Instead, he issued a Proclamation for Suppressing Rebellion and Sedition on August 23, that declared the colonies to be in a state of rebellion. This was the same as a declaration of war against the colonists. He also required British subjects to assist in putting down the rebellion.

Two months after his Proclamation of Rebellion, King George addressed Parliament. He accused the colonists of waging war "for the purpose of establishing an independent empire," blamed them for the "torrent of violence" that had occurred over the years, and vowed to "put a speedy end to these disorders by the most decisive exertions."

Because of the King's Proclamation, many colonists decided to become rebellious Americans instead of remaining loyal British subjects.

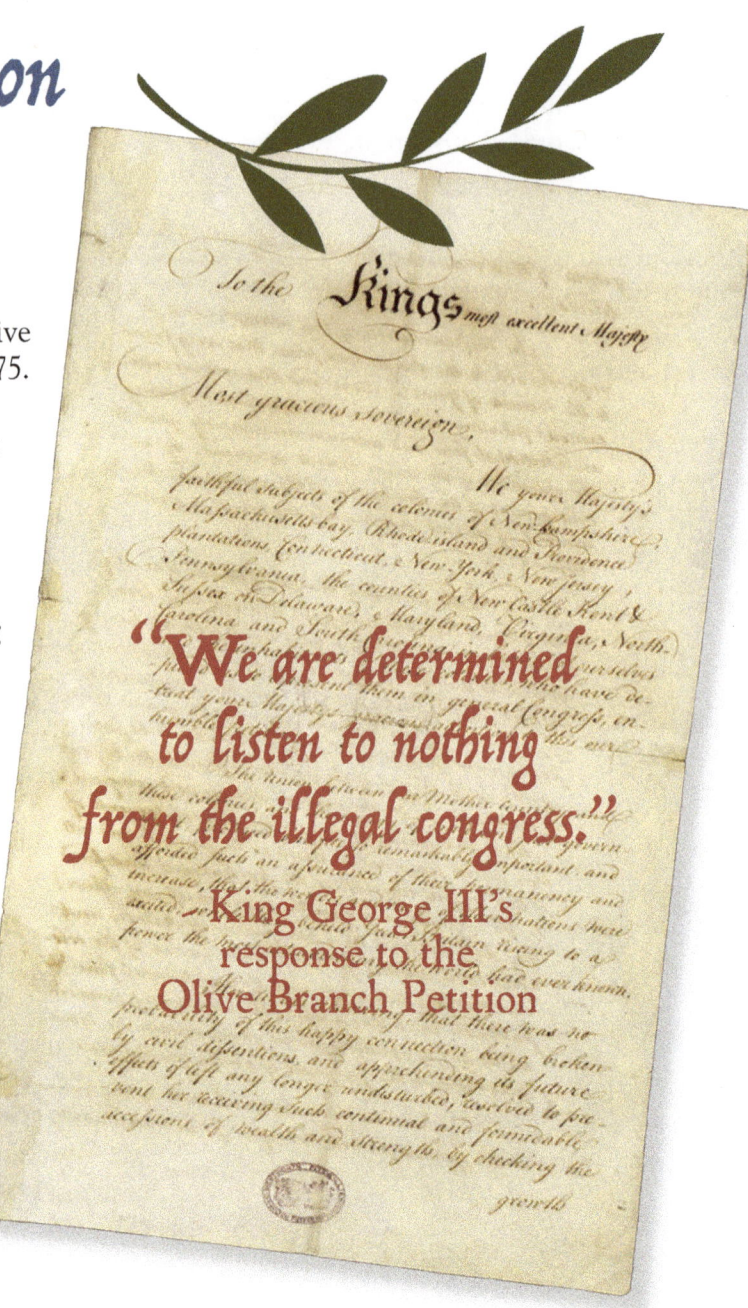

"We are determined to listen to nothing from the illegal congress."
— King George III's response to the Olive Branch Petition

- OCTOBER 13 - AMERICAN ACTION: Congress authorized the Continental Navy.
- OCTOBER 27 - BRITISH ACTION: In his speech to Parliament, King George III ordered Parliament to declare the American colonies to be in a state of rebellion, and authorized military action against them.
- NOVEMBER 29 - AMERICAN ACTION: Congress appointed a secret committee to seek assistance from European nations.
- DECEMBER 23 - BRITISH ACTION: Parliament passed the Prohibitory Act that closed the colonies to all commerce and trade.

Continental Navy Created

A Continental Navy was authorized by the Second Continental Congress on October 13, 1775. Esek Hopkins was named Commander-in-Chief on December 22 and formally organized the Navy. The first fleet consisted of seven ships: two 24-gun frigates, two 14-gun brigs and three schooners. The original purpose was to capture British shipments of arms, equipment and provisions.

The first and the current U.S. Naval Jack flag includes a rattlesnake superimposed across 13 alternating red and white stripes with the motto "Don't Tread On Me."

King George III Closed America's Ports

On December 23, 1775, Parliament passed the Prohibitory Act in retaliation to the growing American revolt against British rule. The Act placed a naval blockade on American ports that stopped the colonies from trading with foreign countries and each other. British ships were exempted. It also authorized that all American ships would be seized and the cargo sold.

Closing the ports was a severe economic blow to the colonies. The ports were important because the economies of each colony were based on the mercantile system. Which meant the colonies provided raw materials, such as rice and tobacco, to Great Britain, and in return Great Britain shipped manufactured goods, such as textiles and ceramics, back to colonial merchants to be sold.

The closing of ports was another offensive action that convinced the public and members of Congress to support American independence.

Congress reacted by issuing letters of marque to American ship owners, which gave them the authority to seize British ships and sell the cargo.

Commanders-in-Chief

Commander-in-chief, American Continental Army

General George Washington
Served: June 1775 - December 1783

Commander-in-chief, Great Britain's Forces

General Thomas Gage
Served: May 1774 - September 1775

Commander-in-chief, Great Britain's Forces

General William Howe
Served: September 1775 - May 1778

Commander-in-chief, Great Britain's Forces

General Henry Clinton
Served: May 1778 - May 1782

Colonials vs. British

1 - A zeal and determination for independence
2 - Good knowledge of terrain and conditions
3 - Fought with guerrilla tactics and straight-line formations
4 - Had one commander-in-chief the entire war
5 - Washington had an efficient spy network
6 - Fewer men on battlefields than Redcoats
7 - Generals were inexperienced and lacked military knowledge
8 - Soldiers were good marksmen but lacked experience, training and equipment
9 - France and Spain assisted by providing financial and military aid
10 - American patriots supported the war but were unreliable some of the time

1 - Only wanted to survive and go home
2 - Little knowledge of terrain and conditions
3 - Fought with centuries old straight-line battle formations
4 - Had three commanders-in-chief during the war
5 - British spy system was not effective
6 - Outnumbered the Americans during most battles
7 - Generals were overconfident and underestimated the Americans
8 - Soldiers were experienced, trained and equipped
9 - British treasury was stretched with a world-wide war
10 - British loyalists kept their sympathies private because they feared harassment

Communications in Times of Emergency

Fast communications in colonial America became more urgent in the years prior to the American Revolution. Pen, paper and messengers on horseback were the only ways to send messages to distant places. As the dispute between the Americans and the British government grew, a faster system was needed.

The Alarm and Muster System was an improved version over the old method. Church bells, drum rolls, alarm guns, bonfires and trumpet calls provided speedier communications among the towns.

The midnight rides of Paul Revere, William Dawes and others on April 19, 1775, activated the Alarm and Muster System which rapidly alerted thousands of Massachusetts's militia to confront the Redcoats as they marched on Lexington and Concord and back to Boston.

Joseph Plumb Martin
Young Patriot Fought 7 Years in Continental Army

Joseph Plumb Martin was one of only a small number of men who fought during the entire American Revolution. The 15-year old first enlisted in the Connecticut militia where he served six months before joining the Continental Army. He participated in battles and faced hardships from New England to Virginia during the seven years (1776-1783) that he fought for America's independence.

Martin began his service as a private and ended the war as a sergeant.

Born in Becket, Massachusetts, in 1760, and at the age of seven, he was sent to live with his affluent grandfather. There he received a good education.

He kept a diary during the war. In 1830, at the age of 70, Martin published his first-hand account of his life as a Continental soldier. It was titled *A Narrative of Some of the Adventures, Dangers and Sufferings of a Revolutionary Soldier*. His accounts of battles and living conditions are very descriptive. The diary is still available today.

He died in Maine on May 2, 1850, at the age of 89.

> George Washington often referred to his men in the Continental Army as "my brave fellows."

Continental Soldiers
The Continental Army at the Beginning

The men who enlisted in the Continental Army after Lexington and Concord were mostly farmers.

When Washington took command in Boston, the Continental Army was not an army. It was a loose, unorganized band of citizen-soldiers and militiamen under the command of local militia leaders.

His first task was to establish military authority and to organize the men into a viable fighting force. Proper procedures to acquire and distribute food and supplies were also essential.

The new Continental soldiers were poorly armed, poorly clothed, poorly fed, poorly paid and woefully unequipped. They ranged in age from young boys to old men. The majority were 18-24.

When volunteers signed up for an enlistment period they were promised a monthly salary: privates $6, sergeants $8 and captains $20. They had to provide their own uniforms, gear and weapons.

Despite the many problems and disadvantages that developed, they were committed to winning independence from Great Britain. They endured hardships that can only be imagined.

American soldiers often went weeks and months without pay

Slaves and free blacks served in the Continental and British armies.

It is estimated that more than 5,000 served on the American side. Peter Salem fought at Lexington and Concord. Salem Poor fought at Bunker Hill. James Lafayette was an American spy.

The freed slaves freely volunteered to serve the American cause, but the enslaved ones did not volunteer. Their masters gave them to the recruiting officers instead of volunteering themselves. A small percentage of slaves received their freedom when the war ended. The majority, however, remained the property of their masters.

The British enticed slaves to volunteer by promising freedom and land to those who would join. When the war ended, many slaves received freedom, but a large number did not. Some 20,000 slaves served the British military.

Slaves Fought for the Americans and the British

Continental Soldier's Equipment

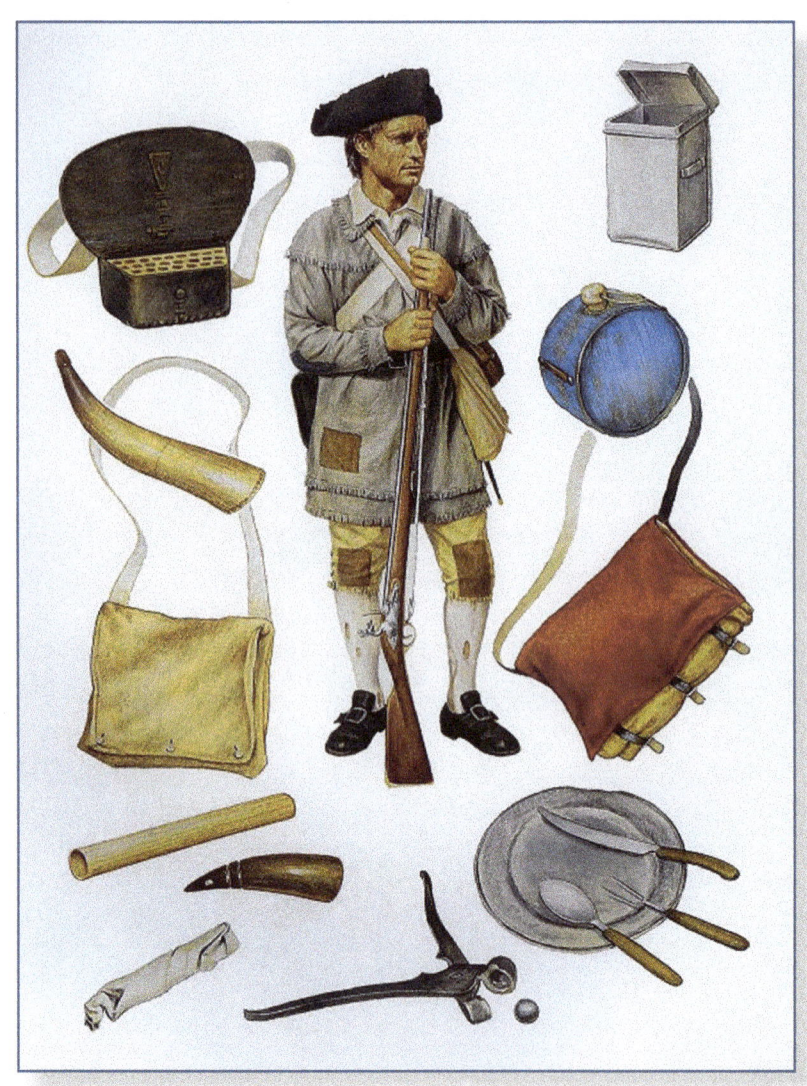

- **MUSKET** that weighed 10.5 pounds and was 58.5 inches long.
- **LEATHER or TIN CARTRIDGE BOX** with 20-30 musket balls, musket tool and flints, carried on the right side.
- **POWDER HORN** for black gun powder.
- **BAYONET** in a leather scabbard attached to a linen or leather shoulder strap, carried on the left side.
- **HAVERSACK**, usually made of linen that carried food and utensils, including a wrought iron fork, pewter or horn spoon, knife, plate and cup.
- **WATER CANTEEN** made of wood, tin or glass.
- **KNAPSACK** for clothing, personal items, blanket, candles and candle holders, and a tinderbox for flint and steel.

Uniforms were important to the armies. Battles fought with black-powder weapons would produce thick smoke making it difficult to see more than a few yards. It was important to distinguish between friends and enemies. Because smoke was usually white, bright colors were used for uniforms. The British wore mostly red uniforms; the French wore uniforms of white and differing shades of blue; and the Americans wore dark blues and browns. Congress did not adopt a Continental uniform until 1779. Soldiers attempted to have clothing similar to each other in the same company or regiment.

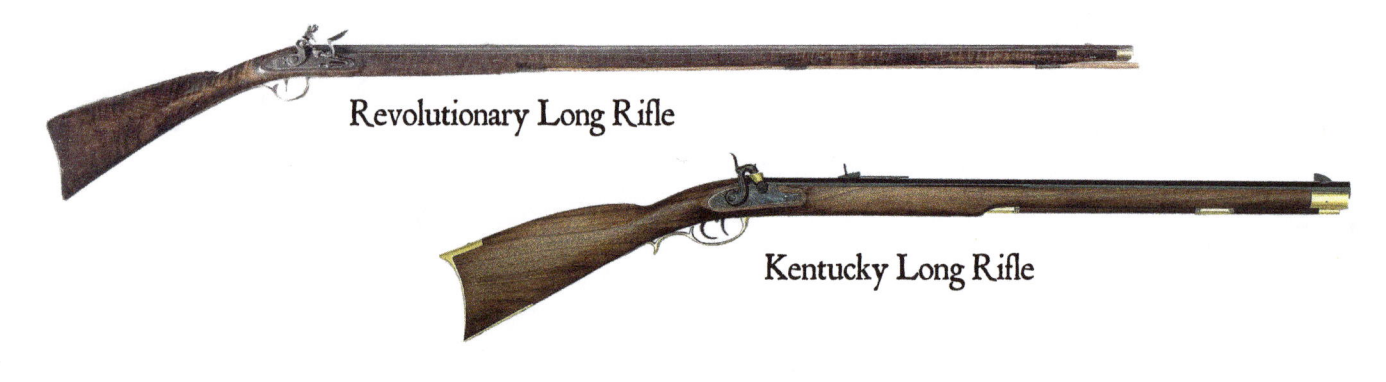

Revolutionary Long Rifle

Kentucky Long Rifle

How to Load a Musket

Continental soldiers could only fire their muskets an average of two times a minute. Loading a musket was a time-consuming process that involved a number of steps. If any step was skipped the musket would not fire or might even explode in their face.

When commanded by a superior officer, here are the procedures to load a musket.
- *Prime and Load* - Position the musket a quarter turn to the right.
- *Handle Cartridge* - Remove a cartridge from the cartridge box. Rip or bite the paper off. Hold the ball and cartridge in the right hand. (A paper cartridge contains a pre-measured amount of black powder and a musket ball.)
- *Prime* - Pull the hammer (or dog-head) back to half cock. Pour a small amount of black powder from the paper cartridge into the priming pan. Close the frizzen and tap the black powder.
- *About* - Lower the musket butt to the ground. Pour the rest of the black powder into the muzzle and add the ball and wadding.
- *Draw Ramrods* - Remove the ramrod from beneath the barrel. Place the ramrod into the barrel and firmly tap the ball and wadding to the bottom of the barrel with two firm taps. Return the ramrod to the channel.
- *Present* - Bring the butt to your shoulder. Aim the weapon in the direction of the enemy. Pull the cock all the way back.
- *Fire* - Pull the trigger back then squeeze to make the weapon discharge.

On the battlefield, it was more efficient to fire muskets in unison rather than individually, because they were unreliable at hitting targets.

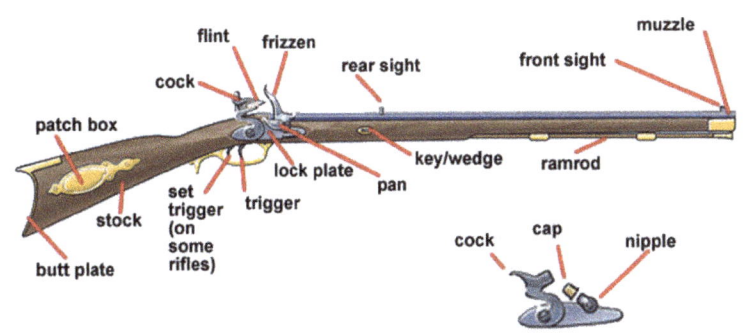

Each man had to provide his own weapon. Most of the time they brought the weapon that was used for protection and to provide food for their families.
- Brown Bess was a muzzle-loading smoothbore musket that was used by the Americans and British. The effective firing range was only 50 to 100 yards, and was not very accurate.
- Charleville Muskets was another popular musket that was imported from France.
- American made muskets were produced by local gunsmiths that were made with reused parts from other weapons.
- American long rifles were developed in the early 1700s for frontiersmen. With a range up to 300 yards they were more accurate than a musket.
- Bayonets were used for close combat when a musket or long rifle could not be reloaded. They were hand forged by local blacksmiths or soldiers.

Charleville Musket

Brown Bess Musket

Independence Flames Grow

1776

- **JANUARY 10** - AMERICAN ACTION: Thomas Paine's *Common Sense* was published in Philadelphia.
- **FEBRUARY 27** - AMERICAN ACTION: 1,000 American patriots defeated 1,600 British loyalists at the Battle of Moore's Creek Bridge in North Carolina.
- **MARCH 4 to 17** - AMERICAN ACTION: American forces captured Dorchester Heights that overlooked Boston harbor.
- **APRIL 6** - AMERICAN ACTION: The Continental Congress declared all American shipping ports open, except for British vessels.
- **APRIL 12** - AMERICAN ACTION: North Carolina's Fourth Provincial Congress adopted the Halifax Resolves that empowered the North Carolina delegates to the Continental Congress to vote for independence.
- **MAY 2** - FRENCH ACTION: French King Louis XVI began providing secret military aid to the American cause for independence. Spain promised to give support.
- **MAY 10** - AMERICAN ACTION: The Continental Congress encouraged the colonies to write constitutions and establish independent governments.

"Common Sense" Changed Minds

One of the most significant events that led to American independence was the publication of *Common Sense* on January 10, 1776. Published anonymously by Thomas Paine, the 50-page pamphlet was signed "Written by an Englishman."

During the first year it sold more than 500,000 copies with 25 separate printings. Paine donated the royalties to the American Continental Army.

Common Sense played a major role in influencing public opinion to support independence. Written in language that even the uneducated people of the time could understand, Paine: (1) ridiculed the idea of a small, island nation ruling a vast continent; (2) presented a powerful argument that independence from British rule was America's only choice; (3) believed that reconciliation was not a good option for Americas; and, (4) outlined the advantages that separation from England would provide. His writing helped people to realize that the actions of King George III and Parliament had already shattered the bonds between the America people and the British government.

Thomas Paine had only lived in America for two years before *Common Sense* was published. Coming from a humble background, he had a hard time finding his place in England. He had been a staymaker, a maker of ladies' corsets and men's vests, a cobbler, a weaver and a tax collector. After his marriage failed, he decided to leave England. Benjamin Franklin, whom he met by happenstance when Franklin was in London, helped him immigrate to Philadelphia, where he found work writing for the *Pennsylvania Magazine*.

"I offer nothing more than simple facts, plain arguments, and common sense."

• • •

"The cause of America is, in a great measure, the cause of all mankind."

– Thomas Paine

General Howe's Goal Was to Crush the Continental Army

The British plan for 1776 was to seize control of New York City and isolate the northern colonies from the southern colonies by taking control of the Hudson River. British Major General William Howe also believed the Continental Army could be crushed with a single battle on Long Island.

Howe began evacuating Boston on March 17. He temporarily moved his army to Halifax, Nova Scotia, where he started making plans to occupy New York City. After a brief stay, he moved 9,300 Redcoats on 130 transport ships to the city. They landed on June 30.

General Washington had anticipated Howe's move to New York and marched the Continental Army where it occupied Manhattan and Long Island. He ordered the construction of Fort Washington and Fort Lee along the Hudson River.

Two months later on August 27, the Battle of Long Island began with British navy cannons bombarding the Americans for five days. At that point, 32,000 British soldiers invaded Manhattan Island and defeated Washington's troops at Kip's Bay – marking the beginning of the seven year British occupation of New York City.

Redcoats were moved ashore to begin the occupation of New York City.

Halifax Resolves - First in Freedom

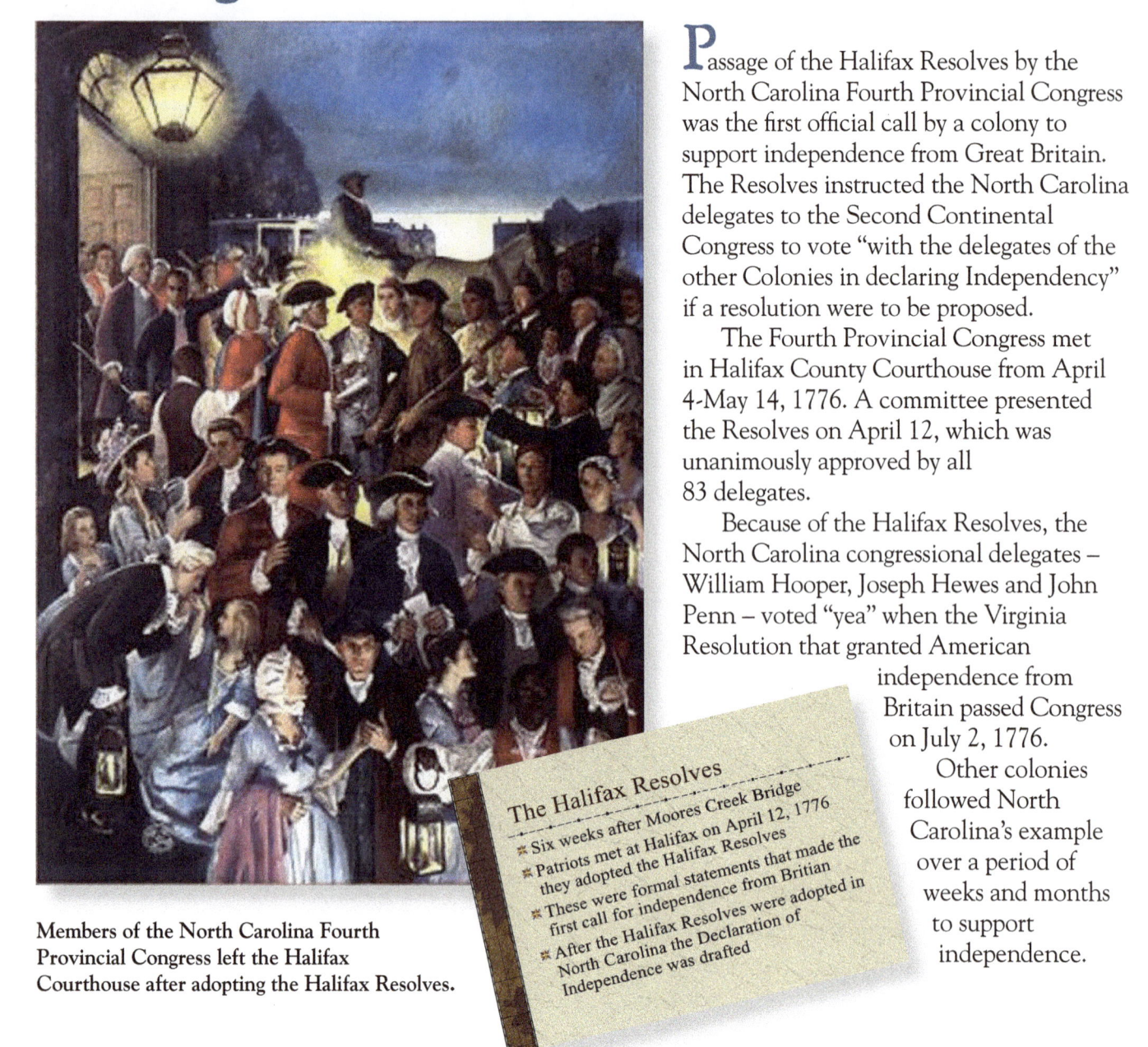

Passage of the Halifax Resolves by the North Carolina Fourth Provincial Congress was the first official call by a colony to support independence from Great Britain. The Resolves instructed the North Carolina delegates to the Second Continental Congress to vote "with the delegates of the other Colonies in declaring Independency" if a resolution were to be proposed.

The Fourth Provincial Congress met in Halifax County Courthouse from April 4-May 14, 1776. A committee presented the Resolves on April 12, which was unanimously approved by all 83 delegates.

Because of the Halifax Resolves, the North Carolina congressional delegates – William Hooper, Joseph Hewes and John Penn – voted "yea" when the Virginia Resolution that granted American independence from Britain passed Congress on July 2, 1776.

Other colonies followed North Carolina's example over a period of weeks and months to support independence.

Members of the North Carolina Fourth Provincial Congress left the Halifax Courthouse after adopting the Halifax Resolves.

The Halifax Resolves
* Six weeks after Moores Creek Bridge Patriots met at Halifax on April 12, 1776 they adopted the Halifax Resolves
* These were formal statements that made the first call for independence from Britian
* After the Halifax Resolves were adopted in North Carolina the Declaration of Independence was drafted

France and Spain Joined American War for Independence

On May 2, 1776, King Louis XVI of France authorized one million livre to purchase arms, munitions, tents and clothing for the American Continental Army. This was the foreign support Congress had been seeking. Two years later, American and French representatives signed the Treaty of Amity and Commerce and the Treaty of Alliance. With the first treaty, France recognized America as an independent nation and promoted trade between the two countries. The Treaty of Alliance united them as allies against Great Britain. During the last years of the war, France provided substantial amounts of military supplies and funds, as well as 12,000 soldiers and 32,000 sailors to fight along side the Americans.

At the urging of American representative John Jay, Spain agreed to provide large amounts of money and naval support that helped defeat the British.

- **JUNE 7** - AMERICAN ACTION: Richard Henry Lee, a Virginia delegate to the Continental Congress, presented the Virginia Resolution that called for independence for the 13 colonies.
- **JUNE 11** - AMERICAN ACTION: In response to the introduction of the Virginia Resolution, Congressional president John Hancock appointed the Committee of Five to write a declaration of independence.
- **JUNE 28** - AMERICAN ACTION: American forces defended Fort Moultrie on Sullivan's Island in Charleston, South Carolina against a British naval attack and inflicted heavy damage on the British fleet.
- **JUNE 28** - AMERICAN ACTION: The Committee of Five presented the Declaration of Independence to Congress.
- **JULY 2** - AMERICAN ACTION: Twelve colonies voted to adopt the Virginia Resolution. The New York delegates abstained from voting.
- **JULY 4** - AMERICAN ACTION: Congress approved the Declaration of Independence. New York was the only colony not to vote.
- **JULY 12** - BRITISH ACTION: Reinforcements arrived: 30 battleships landed at Staten Island with 300 cargo ships, 1,200 cannons, 30,000 soldiers and 10,000 sailors.
- **JULY 12** - BRITISH ACTION: Two British frigates sailed up the Hudson River as a show of force.
- **AUGUST 2** - AMERICAN ACTION: 56 members of Congress signed the Declaration of Independence.

The Resolution That Freed the Colonies

Richard Henry Lee of Virginia followed instructions from the Virginia Convention and introduced the Virginia Resolution to Congress on June 7, 1776.

This resolution declared the Colonies to be free and independent States. It stated: "Resolved, That these United Colonies are, and of right ought to be, free and independent States, that they are absolved from all allegiance to the British Crown, and that all political connection between them and the State of Great Britain is, and ought to be, totally dissolved." This resolution started the chain of events that led to the Declaration of Independence.

The Virginia Convention unanimously approved the resolution on May 15 in Williamsburg, Virginia.

On June 11, President Hancock appointed the Committee of Five to write a declaration of independence.

Consideration of the Virginia Resolution was postponed until July 1 to give delegates time to get instructions from their colonies before voting.

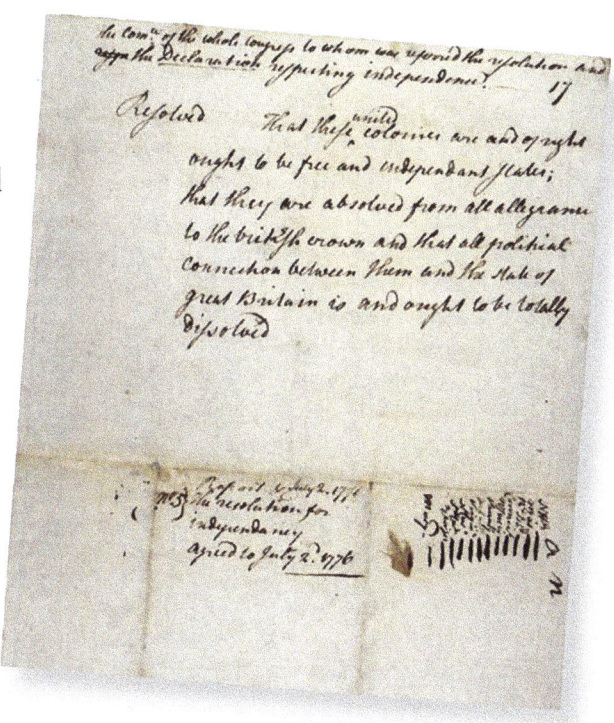

Richard Henry Lee's original copy of the Virginia Resolution.

John Hancock, President of the 2nd Continental Congress, appointed the Committee of Five to write the Declaration.

June 11, 1776

Meeting held at Benjamin Franklin's home

- Excerpt from Jefferson's Masterpiece, pages 1-3

"We were given an important job," added Benjamin Franklin. "Our assignment is to write a statement that clearly sets forth our reasons for breaking ties with the government of Great Britain. We must select the right man to write our declaration of independence."

"There is only one man on this committee or in this Congress who can write the kind of statement we need," answered John Adams as his eyes settled on Thomas Jefferson. "That man is you, Thomas." He turned in his chair so he directly faced Jefferson, who felt uncomfortable by his friend's attention. "We all know you are an experienced and able writer." Adams paused for a brief moment. "Gentlemen, I nominate Thomas for this important job."

Franklin, Roger Sherman and Robert Livingston looked at each other and nodded their heads. "We all agree," Franklin responded.

After a few moments of hesitation, Thomas Jefferson spoke. "I appreciate your confidence, John, but I think the committee should appoint you. Virginia, as you know, recently declared its independence from the British government. My countrymen are now working to establish a new government. I would like to take part by helping to write Virginia's constitution. In fact, I have already made some notes that I plan to take when I go to Williamsburg. John, you should write the declaration. You led the fight to get us this far; you should be the one to write it."

"But . . . you know how important a written declaration of America's independence would be for the colonies," responded Adams. "This is a matter that concerns all the colonies – all the citizens. The new government for Virginia is important, of course, but freedom for all of our people is the most important business at hand.

"You are the best person – the only person – to write our declaration of independence. I urge you to accept." Adams returned to his seat.

Jefferson felt compelled to return to Virginia. "What can be your reasons?" He asked as he looked directly into Adams' eyes.

"Reasons enough," Adams answered. "Reason first: You are a Virginian, and a Virginian ought to appear at the head of this business. Reason second: I am obnoxious, suspected and unpopular. Reason third: You can write ten times better than I can."

All eyes were fixed on Jefferson, who sat with his head bowed. The only sound in the room was the ticking of the grandfather clock that stood beside the window. He raised his head and looked momentarily into the face of each man. They watched as he crossed his arms and cupped his chin with his left hand. He stared at the floor in front of him. More time passed until he scanned the face of each man again. "If you are determined," he finally said, "I will do as well as I can."

Where Jefferson Wrote the Declaration

During his stay in Philadelphia, Thomas Jefferson rented a two room suite on the second floor in the Graff House. He wrote the Declaration of Independence in the parlor on the portable desk he had designed, using the small silver fountain pen he purchased from a Richmond watchmaker. The Graff House was a new residence owned by Jacob Graff, Jr., a local bricklayer.

Portable Desk

Parlor

Silver Fountain Pen

From Subjects to Citizens

- Excerpt from *Jefferson's Masterpiece*, page 30

"Jefferson was almost finished with the middle section that listed the grievances against King George III. He carefully began to write the next to last grievance. 'He . . . has . . . incited . . . treasonable . . . insurrections . . . of . . . our . . . fellow . . . subjects.' He suddenly stopped. 'NO!' He realized, 'Subjects is not the correct word. As a free people, we will not be subjects of the British monarchy any longer. We will be citizens of our own country – a new country.' While the ink was still wet, he used his finger to wipe out the word '*subjects*.' He finished writing the sentence with '*citizens*' inserted."

Jefferson Finished Writing ~ Now It Was Up to Congress

The Committee of Five presented Jefferson's "clean copy" of the Declaration of Independence to the Second Continental Congress on June 28. The images above are Jefferson's original four page "rough draught" that included the edits made by Adams, Franklin and Jefferson.

Independence Depended on One Man's Vote

Being a small colony, Delaware only had three delegates and Caesar Rodney was not present in Congress. He was at home with breathing problems caused by asthma and severe facial cancer. He always wore a green scarf to hide his cancer-scared face.

As debate continued on the Virginia Resolution that would declare the colonies independent, fellow Delaware delegate Thomas McKean sent a messenger to alert Rodney that his vote was necessary to decide Delaware's approval for independence. Knowing the vote of the colonies had to be unanimous, McKean knew that Rodney's vote would be needed to break the deadlock between his vote and George Read's vote – Delaware's third delegate.

The message was delivered, and Rodney began his ride to Philadelphia on July 1. It was a terrible night for a person with his bad health to be out. He made the 80 mile trip by horseback on a violent-stormy night over muddy roads, swollen streams and slippery cobblestone streets.

The tired and mud splattered Rodney arrived on July 2 just in time to cast the deciding vote that gave Delaware's approval to the Virginia Resolution.

Congress Spent Days Editing & Voting
July 2-4, 1776

After 12 colonies approved the Virginia Resolution on July 2, Congress proceeded to the Declaration of Independence. The first order of business was for Secretary Thomson to read the Declaration.

"When he finished reading, Benjamin Harrison suggested that the committee of the whole review the document line-by-line to give each delegate the opportunity to offer any changes they might like to make. 'I know you are as impressed with Jefferson's work as I am. However, we do not want anyone to misunderstand our motives. We want to make certain this declaration is a clear and concise statement that everyone will understand. Mr. Thomson, please begin to read . . . slowly . . . sentence-by-sentence.'

"Thomson stood and moved in front of his worktable. He held the document with both hands, cleared his throat and began to read very slowly and deliberately.

"When in the course . . . of human events . . . it becomes necessary . . . for one people . . . to dissolve the political bands . . . which have connected them . . . with another, . . .

"One by one, the delegates began to make suggestions for changes. Jefferson never attempted to defend his work. He left that to John Adams. Instead, he listened to every word that was said and made notes of the changes.

"However, as the delegates reviewed the declaration, Franklin observed that his young friend was visibly upset by the changes that were being made. So he told Jefferson a story about a friend who wanted to get a sign painted for his new hatter's shop. . . .

"This little story amused Jefferson. He thanked his friend for understanding his feelings. 'But, I am afraid our friends are doing the same thing to the declaration that happened to the hatter's sign. It is being mutilated. Nothing will be left when they finish.'"

Changes, additions and deletions to the text continued onto July 3.

"By late afternoon, the delegates were ready to consider the last offense – the slavery clause that John Adams had warned Jefferson about when he read the draft for the first time on June 24. . . .

"In very strong language, Jefferson had condemned the slave trade and criticized King George III for protecting it. Over the years, some colonies had passed laws to reduce or ban the importation of slaves, but the king always vetoed them because of the revenues his government received. . . .

"Speaking on behalf of the South Carolina and Georgia delegates, Edward Rutledge argued that: 'Slave labor is essential to the economies of our colonies. . . . Unless this section is removed, we have no other choice but to vote against ratification of the declaration.'"

Editing the Declaration continued on July 4.

"Finally, when it was obvious their minds were not going to be changed, Jefferson very reluctantly gave his approval for the slave clause to be omitted. Congress then turned its attention to editing the last three paragraphs. When that was completed, President Hancock directed Secretary Thomson to read the edited Declaration aloud.

"The room remained silent when Thomson finished. No one spoke for what seemed like a long time. Hancock broke the silence by telling the delegates that it was time for them to vote on accepting the Declaration of Independence as amended. . . .

"A short time later when all the votes had been cast and counted, Hancock stood, looked over at Jefferson, the two Adamses and Franklin, and gave them a big grin. At a few minutes past two o'clock Hancock proudly announced: 'Fellow delegates, 12 colonies have agreed to the written Declaration of Independence; New York has abstained. I am proud to announce that the Declaration of Independence by the representatives of the United States of America has been approved.'"

- Excerpts from *Jefferson's Masterpiece*, pages 73-74, 79-80, 85 and 88-89

Six Parts of the Declaration of Independence

The Declaration of Independence was a protest document against King George III and it provided principles to establish a new independent country.

1. PREAMBLE - Stated that the purpose of the Declaration is to "declare" the "causes" that impel the colonies to separate from the British Empire. IT BEGINS: "When in the Course of human events, it becomes necessary for one people to dissolve the political bands which have connected them with another, and to assume among the powers of the earth, the separate and equal station to which the Laws of Nature and of Nature's God entitle them, a decent respect to the opinions of mankind requires that they should declare the causes which impel them to the separation. . . ."

2. STATEMENT OF BELIEFS - Established that all men have certain rights. IT BEGINS: "We hold these truths to be self-evident, that all men are created equal, that they are endowed by their Creator with certain unalienable Rights, that among these are Life, Liberty and the pursuit of Happiness. . . ."

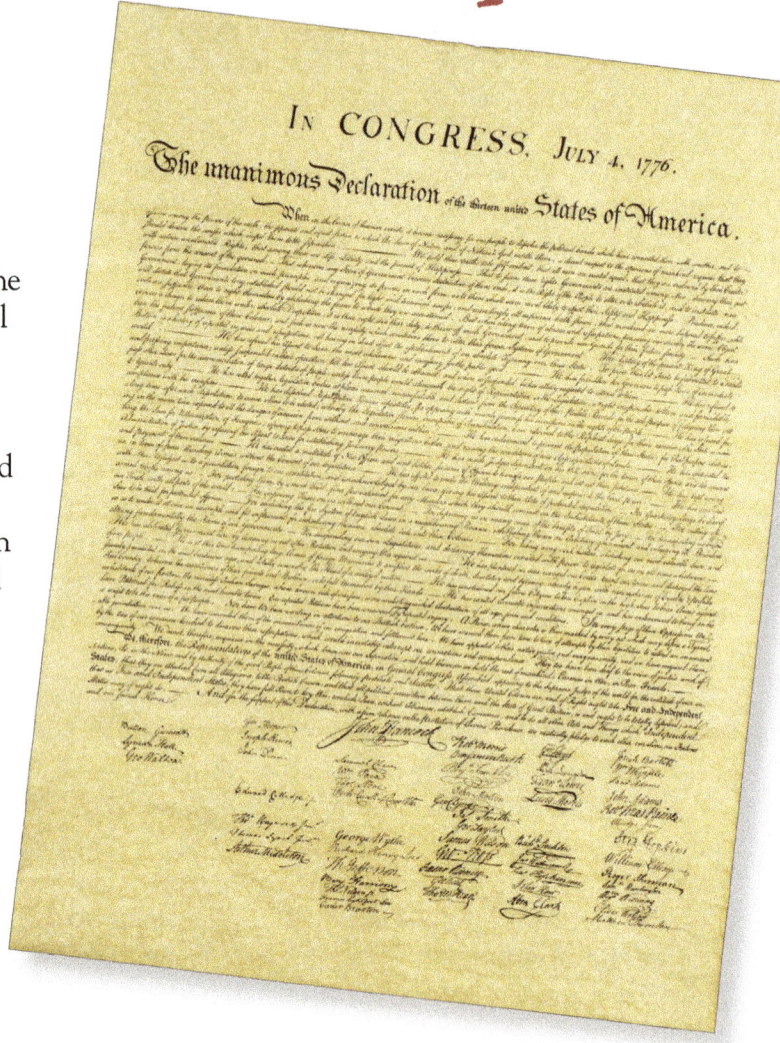

3. COMPLAINTS AGAINST THE KING - Listed 27 grievances the colonists had against King George III and his government. IT BEGINS: "To prove this, let Facts be submitted to a candid World. . . ."

4. ATTEMPTS TO REDRESS GRIEVANCES - Recounted the colonists' efforts to allow the King to remedy their grievances. IT BEGINS: "In every stage of these Oppressions We have Petitioned for Redress in the most humble terms: Our repeated Petitions have been answered only by repeated injury. A Prince whose character is thus marked by every act which may define a Tyrant, is unfit to be the ruler of a free people. . . ."

5. ANNOUNCEMENT OF INDEPENDENCE - Declared that the 13 American colonies are free and independence states. IT BEGINS: "We, therefore, the Representatives of the United States of America, in General Congress, Assembled, appealing to the Supreme Judge of the world for the rectitude of our intentions, do, in the Name, and by Authority of the good People of these Colonies, solemnly publish and declare, That these United Colonies are, and of Right ought to be Free and Independent States; . . ."

6. SIGNATURES - The delegates to the Second Continental Congress signed their approval of the Declaration.

July 4, 1776

How the Delegates Voted

"Secretary Charles Thomson began the roll call in the north with New Hampshire and moved south to Georgia. Each colony had one vote and the majority vote of that colony's representatives determined the vote for the colony. When the name of each delegate was announced, the delegate would stand and say either 'yea' or 'nay.'"

- Excerpt from *Jefferson's Masterpiece*, page 71

Nothing of importance this day.

July 4, 1776
Diary of King George III

Little did the King know that the colonies
- now states -
had declared independence from his rule.

Independence Decisions Had to be Unanimous

The congressional delegates agreed that all issues concerning independence from Great Britain had to be unanimous. For that reason the Declaration's subtitle reads: "The unanimous Declaration of the thirteen United States of America, . . ."

1st Printed Copies of the Declaration

John Dunlap, the official printer for Congress, was given an order on the afternoon of July 4 to print copies of the Declaration of Independence for delivery the next morning. He and his staff worked through the night to handset the type, proofread their work, print and allow adequate time for each sheet to dry before they were delivered. It is estimated that he printed and delivered 200 copies the next morning. These prints are known as the "Dunlap Broadsides." Twenty-four copies are believed to exist today.

July 9, 1776

Declaration Read to the Continental Troops

George Washington's General Orders to the Continental Army instructing them to assemble for a reading of the Declaration of Independence in New York.

"The Honorable Continental Congress, impelled by the dictates of duty, policy and necessity, having been pleased to dissolve the Connection which subsisted between this Country, and Great Britain, and to declare the United Colonies of North America, free and independent States: The several brigades are to be drawn up this evening on their respective Parades, at Six OClock, when the declaration of Congress, shewing the grounds and reasons of this measure, is to be read with an audible voice.

"The General hopes this important Event will serve as a fresh incentive to every officer, and soldier, to act with Fidelity and Courage, as knowing that now the peace and safety of this Country depends (under God) solely on the success of our arms: And that he is now in the service of a State, possessed of sufficient power to reward his merit, and advance him to the highest Honors of a free Country." *

* Original 18th century spelling, punctuation and capitalization in this quote have been retained.

"General Washington rode his horse, Nelson, to the parade grounds where the troops were assembled. The Continental Army was only miles away from the British troops stationed in New York City.

"When he arrived, everyone stood at attention – their eyes were focused on their beloved commander. Washington slowly walked his horse to where his officers were standing. Alexander Hamilton reached up and handed Washington the Declaration.

"Washington positioned Nelson in front of his army. His voice rang loud as he read America's Declaration of Independence to the multitude of men.

"A stunned silence continued when the reading stopped. Suddenly, thousands of excited voices broke out in shouts of 'HUZZAH! . . . HUZZAH! . . . HUZZAH! . . . HUZZAH!' Washington proudly watched as his men celebrated."

A large number of New Yorkers learned about the scheduled reading and stood on the sidelines to listen and rejoice.

- Excerpt from *Jefferson's Masterpiece*, pages 104-105

THE LONDON CHRONICLE

"New York, July 11: On Wednesday last, the declaration of independence was read at the head of each brigade of the continental army, posted at and near New York, and every where received with loud huzzahs, and the utmost demonstrations of joy."

- *London Chronicle*
September 26, 1776

August 2, 1776 - The Declaration was Signed

The Declaration was signed on August 2, 1776, by the 56 congressmen who had enacted the resolution that liberated the colonies, and approved the document that created the United States of America.

"At President John Hancock's direction, Secretary Thomson stood and began to call the roll. The delegates from the New England colonies were the first to be called – New Hampshire, Massachusetts, Connecticut and Rhode Island. . . ."

When called, each man walked to President Hancock's desk and signed his name to America's birth certificate.

"The Declaration of Independence was now official. America was now embarked on the road to freedom. The first step had been completed – independence had been declared. The second and final step was to win a military victory over the superior British forces. Then, and only then, would America be able to establish an independent government for the United States of America."

- Excerpt from *Jefferson's Masterpiece*, pages 111 & 115

> "Advice is received that the Congress resolved upon independence the 4th of July; and, it is said, have declared war against Great Britain in form."
> - *London Chronicle*, August 13, 1776

"For the support of this declaration, with a firm reliance on the protection of divine Providence, we mutually pledge to each other our Lives, our Fortunes and our sacred Honor."

— Declaration of Independence

Signers Suffered Consequences for Supporting the Declaration

Everyone who signed the Declaration understood the risk they were taking. The British government had announced that each man who supported the Declaration of Independence was a traitor, and the penalty was hanging.

"We must all hang together," said Benjamin Franklin jokingly as he signed the Declaration, "or assuredly we shall all hang separately."

Their signatures were confirming the last sentence in the Declaration: "And for the support of this declaration, with a firm reliance on the protection of Divine Providence, we mutually pledge to each other our lives, our fortunes and our sacred honor."

Many signers suffered from British persecution in the months and years that followed. Their family members were seized and imprisoned, and some even died as a result of the experience; homes and estates were invaded, looted and burned; livestock and farm equipment were stolen; crops and timberland were burned; and one delegate's wife died while he was in hiding and he never saw any of his 13 children again.

Captain Jack Jouett of the Virginia militia saved Thomas Jefferson and his household on June 3, 1781, from being captured by Lieutenant Colonel Banastre Tarleton's Loyalist Dragoons.

Focus of War Changed

After the Declaration of Independence was approved, the war became a battle for American independence.

Before the Declaration of Independence, the purpose was to:
- Defend the colonies against the British military;
- Restore rights King George III and Parliament had taken from the colonists; and
- Find ways to make peace with the British government.

- **AUGUST 27 to 29 - BRITISH ACTION:** General William Howe led 15,000 Redcoats against Washington's army in the Battle of Long Island. Outnumbered two to one, the Americans suffered a severe defeat.
- **SEPTEMBER 11 - AMERICAN & BRITISH ACTION:** A peace conference was held on Staten Island between British and American representatives. The conference failed because General Howe demanded that Congress revoke the Declaration of Independence.
- **SEPTEMBER 16 - AMERICAN ACTION:** After evacuating New York City, Washington's army repulsed a British attack during the Battle of Harlem Heights.
- **SEPTEMBER 26 - AMERICAN ACTION:** Congress appointed Thomas Jefferson, Benjamin Franklin and Silas Dean to negotiate treaties with European countries.
- **OCTOBER 28 - AMERICAN ACTION:** Washington's army suffered heavy casualties at the Battle of White Plains.
- **NOVEMBER 16 to 20 - BRITISH ACTION:** British forces won victories at Fort Washington in Manhattan and Fort Lee in New Jersey.
- **DECEMBER 11 - AMERICAN ACTION:** Washington moved his troops across the Delaware River into Pennsylvania. The Continental Congress abandoned Philadelphia and relocated in Baltimore.
- **DECEMBER 25 to 26 - AMERICAN ACTION:** On Christmas night, General Washington moved his troops across the frozen Delaware River into New Jersey. They defeated a force of Hessians at Trenton during a surprise morning raid.

America's Last King

In the beginning King George III wanted to replace the debt his government had incurred during the French and Indian War. He also wanted to avoid conflicts with the Indians in the western territory that now belonged to England.

As time passed, his motive was to keep the American colonies as a member of the British Empire.

He, along with Parliament and his ministers, restricted, penalized, controlled, bullied and taxed the American colonists to the point where they demanded independence.

He made his first public comments about the Declaration of Independence to Parliament on October 31, 1776. The king was not pleased. He made harsh comments about the Declaration and the revolutionary leaders.

He told the members of Parliament, "But so daring and desperate is the spirit of those leaders, whose object has always been dominion and power, that they have now openly renounced all allegiance to the crown, and all political connection with this country. . . . and have presumed to set up their rebellious Confederacies for Independent States."

He said it was necessary to continue the battle.

In the end, King George III became America's last king.

King George III at age 33 wearing his General Officer's coat with the ribbons and star of the Garter. Artist: Johann Zoffany in 1771

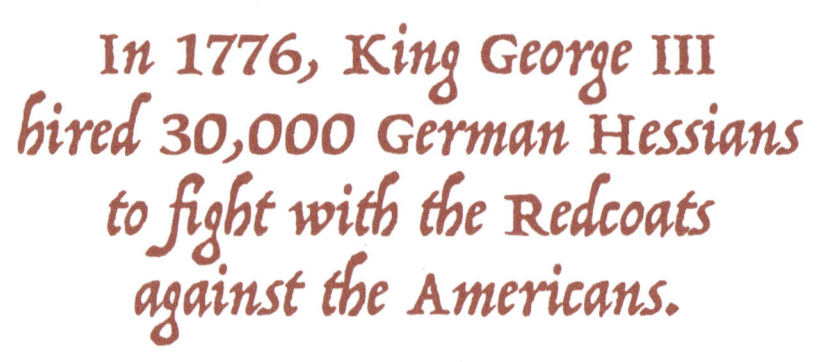

In 1776, King George III hired 30,000 German Hessians to fight with the Redcoats against the Americans.

Washington Caught Hessians Off-Guard Christmas Night

General Washington led his Continental Army across the frozen Delaware River on Christmas night of 1776 and attacked 1,400 Hessians garrisoned at Trenton, New Jersey. It was a difficult and dangerous crossing that took longer and was more difficult than Washington had anticipated.

The sleepy Hessians were caught off-guard during the early morning of December 26 and were completely surrounded. Since they had partied and were drunk from their Christmas celebration, they were slow in getting up and preparing for battle. They surrendered after a short battle that killed 22, wounded 83, with more than 1,000 captured. The American casualties were light – 2 killed and 5 wounded.

This victory was a big morale boost for the Continental soldiers, and a large supply of muskets, bayonets, swords, cannons, and other supplies were captured. It was good news for the colonists too.

Redcoats Go Into High Gear

1777

- **JANUARY 3** - AMERICAN ACTION: Washington's Continental Army defeated the British at Princeton, New Jersey, and drove them back toward New Brunswick.
- **JANUARY 6** - AMERICAN ACTION: General Washington marched the Continental Army to Morristown, New Jersey, where they set up winter camp.
- **MARCH 12** - AMERICAN ACTION: The Continental Congress returned to Philadelphia from Baltimore after the American victory in New Jersey.
- **APRIL 27** - AMERICAN ACTION: American troops, under the command of Benedict Arnold, defeated British forces at Ridgefield, Connecticut.
- **JUNE 14** - AMERICAN ACTION: Congress authorized the first American flag with 13 stars and stripes.
- **JUNE 17** - BRITISH ACTION: A British force, led by General John Burgoyne, invaded the American colonies from Canada by sailing toward Lake Champlain. They linked up with General Howe's forces that were heading north from New York City. The plan was to cut off New England from the rest of the colonies.
- **JULY 6** - BRITISH ACTION: After a five day British siege, General John Burgoyne's troops stunned the Americans when they captured Fort Ticonderoga on Lake Champlain. The loss of the fort's military supplies, which were needed by Washington's forces, was a tremendous blow to American morale.
- **JULY 23** - BRITISH ACTION: British General William Howe, with 15,000 soldiers, sailed from New York to the Chesapeake Bay to capture Philadelphia. Howe decided to go to Philadelphia instead of sailing north to support General Burgoyne's mission.

First United States Flags

The Grand Union Flag also known as the Continental Colors, Congress Flag, Cambridge Flag, and the First Navy Ensign is considered to be America's first national flag. This flag was used during the years when the colonists acknowledged their allegiance to Great Britain and hoped their differences could be reconciled.

On June 14, 1777, the Continental Congress passed the first Flag Act: "Resolved, That the flag of the United States be made of thirteen stripes, alternate red and white; that the union be thirteen stars, white in a blue field, representing a new Constellation." This remained the official Star Spangled Banner until 1795 when two states joined the union.

- **JULY 27 - AMERICAN ACTION:** Marquis de Lafayette, 19-year old French aristocrat, arrived in Philadelphia and volunteered to serve in the Continental Army without pay.
- **AUGUST 16 - AMERICAN ACTION:** Vermont militiamen aided by Massachusetts troops defeated a detachment of 800 German Hessians at the Battle of Bennington.
- **SEPTEMBER 11 - AMERICAN ACTION:** In the Battle of Brandywine, Washington's main Army of 10,500 men were forced to retreat toward Philadelphia by General Howe's troops. Both sides suffered heavy losses.
- **SEPTEMBER 26 - BRITISH ACTION:** British forces occupied Philadelphia. **AMERICAN ACTION:** Congress relocated to York, Pennsylvania.

THE FIRST MEETING OF WASHINGTON AND LAFAYETTE.
Philadelphia, August 3rd 1777.

"Liberty now has a country."
– Marquis de Lafayette

Lafayette Became Washington's Confidant

A 19-year old French aristocrat became a major general on George Washington's staff as well as the son Washington never had.

Because the Marquis de Lafayette became captivated by the American Revolution, he traveled to America with the goal to volunteer his services to the Americans without pay. Recognizing that his wealth and French connections might benefit America's fight for independence, Congress commissioned him a major general on July 31, 1777.

History reports that Lafayette used his own money to pay for his staffs' salaries, uniforms and muskets.

Although he had never seen battle, Lafayette experienced his first action at the Battle of Brandywine. He later commanded Continental troops at Valley Forge and chased British General Charles Cornwallis' army across Virginia and into Yorktown. He was one of three division commanders during the Siege of Yorktown.

Lafayette and Washington remained close after the war. Because of his relationship, Lafayette named his only son George Washington Lafayette.

Loss at Brandywine Prolonged the Revolution

British Generals William Howe and Charles Cornwallis launched a full scale attack on General George Washington's forces and the patriot outpost at Brandywine Creek, near Philadelphia, on September 11, 1777. The generals skillfully split their army into two divisions.

Washington was surprised and unprepared for the attack. The dense morning fog made it difficult for Washington and his officers to see the advancing British troops. Considering the circumstances, the Americans were able to slow the British advance, but being outnumbered 18,000 to 11,000 with the possibility of being surrounded, Washington ordered a retreat.

At the end of the day, the Americans suffered more than 1,100 killed, wounded and captured while the British casualties were in the 600 range. The patriots also had to abandon most of their cannons because their artillery horses were killed or wounded during the fighting.

The Continental Army marched north and camped at Germantown, Pennsylvania, while the British army marched to Philadelphia and occupied the city without any opposition. The Continental Congress had to flee to nearby Lancaster and later to York, Pennsylvania.

Losing the battle and Philadelphia were major blows to American morale. But, once again, Washington had prolonged the fight for independence and saved his army for another day and another battle.

George Washington May Have Escaped Death

During the Battle of Brandywine Creek, a detachment of British marksmen were hiding in the woods waiting for American officers. Major Patrick Ferguson, commander of the loyalist forces at Kings Mountain in 1780, commanded the snipers. He instructed three of his snipers to fire at any American officers that came into view. After a few minutes, Ferguson changed his mind and ordered them not to shoot.

An American officer later rode across the field with other soldiers. Ferguson shouted at him. The officer turned and looked at Ferguson and then rode away. The next day Ferguson learned that the American officer most likely was George Washington.

Major Patrick Ferguson was the inventor of the Ferguson rifle, one of the first breech-loading rifles. It was used briefly by the British during the American Revolution.

- **OCTOBER 7 to 17 - AMERICAN ACTION:** The victory over General John Burgoyne's army at the Battle of Saratoga was an important American victory. The British suffered 600 casualties compared to American losses of 150. Ten days later, Burgoyne's army of 5,700 men surrendered.
- **NOVEMBER 15 - AMERICAN ACTION:** Congress adopted the Articles of Confederation that established America's first national government.
- **DECEMBER 19 - AMERICAN ACTION:** General Washington established winter quarters for his Continental soldiers at Valley Forge, Pennsylvania.
AMERICAN ACTION: The Continental Congress selected John Adams and Benjamin Franklin to go to Paris to attempt to get French support for the American Revolution.

Battle of Saratoga was a Major Win for America

From late September into the first week of October, General Gate's American army was positioned between Burgoyne's army and Albany, New York. On October 7, Burgoyne took the offensive. Both armies crashed together south of the town of Saratoga, and Burgoyne's army was broken. When the fighting ended, 86 percent of Burgoyne's army was captured.

The victory gave new life to the American cause at a critical time. Americans had just suffered a major setback at the Battle of Brandywine Creek as well as the news of the fall of Philadelphia to the British.

One American soldier declared, "It was a glorious sight to see the haughty Britons march out and surrender their arms to an army which but a little before they despised and called paltroons."

The decisive American victory gave France the confidence it needed to enter the war as an American ally. France's financial and military assistance provided a great boost to America's successes.

The Battle of Saratoga was a turning point of the Revolutionary War.

Two key facts illustrate the scope of the victory: (1) 5,895 British and Hessian troops surrendered their arms on October 17. (2) The size of General Burgoyne's expeditionary force was reduced by 86 percent, compared to when they triumphantly marched into New York from Canada during the early summer.

The Continental Congress celebrated the Saratoga victory by issuing a proclamation that called for a national day "for solemn Thanksgiving and praise." Churches complied by holding services in all the colonies.

Articles of Confederation Led to U.S. Constitution

On November 15, the Continental Congress adopted the Articles of Confederation – the forerunner to the Constitution of the United States of America.

After the Declaration of Independence was approved, members of Congress realized that a national government was needed. After months of debate, the Articles of Confederation were approved.

The Articles created a loose confederation of 13 sovereign states with a weak national government. The new government did not have an executive branch or a court system, and congress had limited powers.

Over time, the Articles proved to be unsatisfactory, which led to the establishment of our current federal government, under authority of the Constitution of the United States.

"Rough Sailing Ahead?"

Washington Established Winter Quarters

The Continental Army ended 1777 with a pivotal victory at Saratoga after losing battles at Brandywine, Paoli and Germantown.

Philadelphia was now in British hands and Congress had moved to York, Pennsylvania.

On December 19, 1777, General Washington marched his 12,000 hungry, sick and tired men into Valley Forge for winter camp. Valley Forge was located about 20 miles from Philadelphia. The site was picked because of its strategic location near Philadelphia, its defensible position, and the available firewood and water.

One of Washington's first orders was for the men to build 12' x 12' log cabins with a chimney and 12 bunks. Trenches and earthen fortifications were also built around the camp to defend against possible Redcoat attacks.

It soon became apparent to Washington that it would a miserable winter. Many soldiers were already without shoes, coats and blankets. Also, he knew the prospect of being resupplied was very slim. He was distressed knowing that large numbers of soldiers would get sick and die from the bitter winter, diseases and lack of adequate food. Unfortunately, conditions grew worse than he expected.

Part of the problem was that many local farmers withheld food and grain from the army and sold it instead to the British for higher prices paid in gold and silver. Congress was also unable to provide a steady flow of money for army supplies. Lastly, many states did not have the resources to help soldiers from their states.

An estimated 2,000 men died that winter at Valley Forge.

On December 23, 1777, Washington reported to Congress that his soldiers had to "occupy a cold bleak hill and sleep under frost and Snow without Cloaths or Blankets."

Washington's Headquarters Marquee

When on the battlefield, George Washington used marquees for his headquarters: office, dining and sleeping accommodations. Several of the 20' x 15' oval-shaped tents were needed during the war.

The marquees were made of duck canvas with red scalloped edges. Transportable floors were made of wooden slats that provided protection from water and mud.

They were used whenever private homes or other structures were not available. Sometimes those homes were large enough to provide working and sleeping space for some of his staff.

This original headquarters tent can be seen at the Museum of the American Revolution in Philadelphia. It has been carefully preserved.

This 13 star flag flew at Washington's headquarters during the war. The 6 pointed stars are similar to the three silver stars on his uniform.

Washington Returned General Howe's Dog

After the Battle of Germantown in Pennsylvania on October 4, 1777, a small dog was seen running around the battlefield. The dog followed the Americans at the close of the battle.

Some battle weary Americans captured the dog and saw from his collar that he belonged to British General William Howe. They took the dog to Washington's headquarters, who welcomed the dog and his guardians.

After examining the dog and reading the inscription on the collar, Washington directed Alexander Hamilton, his aide-de-camp, to write a note to General Howe and arrange for the dog and note to be delivered.

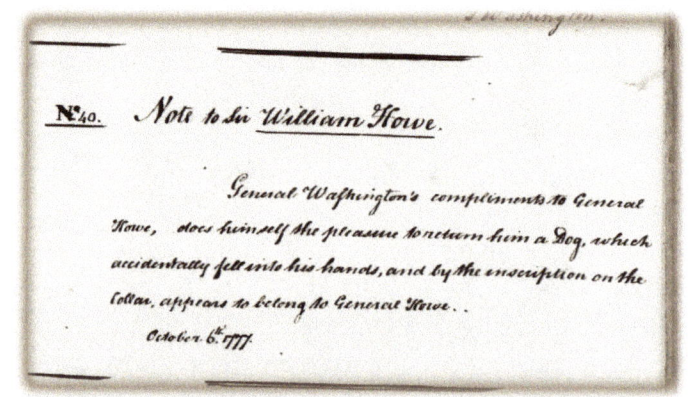

Written in Alexander Hamilton's hand, the note was copied into Washington's letter book that his aides-de-camp kept for his archives.

On October 6, the dog and note were delivered to General Howe's battlefield headquarters. The two-sentence note read: "General Washington's compliments to General Howe. He does himself the pleasure to return him a dog, which accidentally fell into his hands, and by the inscription on the Collar appears to belong to General Howe".

It was reported that General Howe was grateful to General Washington for returning Lila, his fox terrier.

France Recognized America as a Nation

1778

- **FEBRUARY 6** - AMERICAN & FRENCH ACTION: Representatives signed the Treaty of Amity and Commerce and the Treaty of Alliances that provided military supplies to the Continental Army and established trade between the two countries.
- **FEBRUARY 23** - AMERICAN ACTION: Baron von Steuben of Prussia arrived at Valley Forge to join the Continental Army.
- **MARCH 16** - BRITISH ACTION: Parliament sent a Peace Commission to Philadelphia to negotiate with Congress. The commissioners offered to grant all of Congress' demands, except for independence. Congress rejected the peace terms.
- **JUNE 18** - BRITISH ACTION: Fearing a blockade by French ships, British General Henry Clinton withdrew his troops from Philadelphia and marched across New Jersey toward New York City. AMERICAN ACTION: The Americans re-occupied Philadelphia.
- **JUNE 19** - AMERICAN ACTION: Washington sent six brigades to intercept General Clinton's forces.
- **JUNE 27 and 28** - AMERICAN & BRITISH ACTION: American troops fought General Clinton's forces to a standoff at the Battle of Monmouth in New Jersey.
- **JULY 2** - AMERICAN ACTION: Congress returned to Philadelphia.
- **AUGUST 8** - AMERICAN & FRENCH ACTION: An American land force and French ships attempted to conduct a combined siege against Newport, Rhode Island. Bad weather and delays of land troops resulted in failure.
- **DECEMBER 29** - BRITISH ACTION: British forces started a major southern campaign by capturing Savannah, Georgia. A month later they captured Augusta, Georgia.

Winning Partnership Formed

Two treaties signed between America and France on February 6, 1778, provided critical aid in America's fight for independence. The Treaty of Amity and Commerce recognized the United States as an independent nation and established a commercial alliance between the two allies. The Treaty of Alliance provided valuable military supplies to the Continental Army.

France had secretly been furnishing assistance since 1775.

The French government was eager to help America against its old enemy. The rivalry between France and England was centuries old, including France's loss to the British during the French and Indian War.

The American victory at the Battle of Saratoga in October 1777 convinced French leaders that the Americans could defeat the Redcoats with French help. In fact, French soldiers and ships would provide the winning edge three years later when the British surrendered at Yorktown.

Royal Standard of the King of France 1778

Baron von Steuben Arrived at Valley Forge

The arrival of Baron von Steuben on February 23, 1778, with his offer of service brightened the spirits throughout the camp. Washington gladly accepted Steuben's proposal to train the Continental Army – Prussian-style. He did not speak English.

First, Major General Steuben wrote a training manual. Then he trained a "model company" of 100 men using Prussian style drills. Each man from the model company then trained another group who trained another brigade. This process continued until every able bodied man was trained to be a skilled and confident soldier.

When the Continental Army marched out of Valley Forge with a renewed spirit on June 19, 1778, Washington knew his disciplined, revitalized, reorganized, and highly trained army was better prepared than ever to face the British army. The officers and soldiers felt a renewed sense of confidence and determination. They were now focused on completing their mission.

British Forces Raided & Burned

1779

- **MAY 10** - BRITISH ACTION: British troops burned Portsmouth and Norfolk, Virginia.
- **JULY 5 to 11** - BRITISH ACTION: Loyalists raided coastal towns in Connecticut, burning Fairfield, Norwalk and the ships in New Haven harbor.
- **JULY 10** - BRITISH ACTION: American naval ships from Massachusetts were destroyed by the British while attempting to take the loyalist stronghold of Castine, Maine.
- **SEPTEMBER 3 to OCTOBER 28** - AMERICAN ACTION: Americans suffered a major defeat while attacking the British at Savannah, Georgia.
- **OCTOBER 17** - AMERICAN ACTION: Washington established winter quarters at Morristown, New Jersey.
- **DECEMBER 26** - BRITISH ACTION: British General Clinton and 8,000 troops sailed from New York to Charleston, South Carolina.

Both Sides Struggled for Victory
1780

- **MARCH 2 to MAY 12** - BRITISH ACTION: The British Siege of Charleston began when 14 warships anchored in Charleston Harbor. For six weeks American Major General Benjamin Lincoln's army of 5,466 infantry and militia defended Charleston. On May 11 they were forced to surrender.
- **JUNE 11** - AMERICAN ACTION: A new constitution for Massachusetts was approved that stated, "all men are born free and equal," including black slaves.
- **JUNE 23** - AMERICAN ACTION: American forces defeated the British at the Battle of Springfield in New Jersey.
- **JULY 11** - FRENCH ACTION: 6,000 French soldiers arrived at Newport, Rhode Island. Because of the British blockade, they remained there for nearly a year.
- **AUGUST 16** - BRITISH ACTION: The Americans suffered a major defeat at the Battle of Camden in South Carolina. When the battle started, the Americans outnumbered the British two to one, but the weakened, sick American soldiers were unable to fight.
- **AUGUST 18** - BRITISH ACTION: British forces under Lieutenant-Colonel Banastre Tarleton defeated an American militia company at the Battle of Fishing Creek in South Carolina. This opened a route for General Cornwallis to invade North Carolina.
- **SEPTEMBER 21** - BRITISH ACTION: American General Benedict Arnold conspired to turn over West Point to the British. The plot failed and he defected to the British side and became a British officer and led troops against Americans.
- **OCTOBER 7** - AMERICAN ACTION: American frontiersmen defeated British Major Patrick Ferguson and his army of loyalists at the Battle of Kings Mountain.
- **OCTOBER 12** - BRITISH ACTION: After the defeat at Kings Mountain, General Cornwallis abandoned Charlotte and moved his army to South Carolina.
- **OCTOBER 14** - AMERICAN ACTION: General Nathanael Greene was named the new commander of the Southern Army, replacing General Gates. He began a strategy to rally popular support and wear down the British military by leading them on a six-month chase through South Carolina, North Carolina and Virginia.

On March 2, 1780, the British siege of Charleston began when 14 warships anchored in Charleston Harbor. The siege ended on May 12 when American Major General Lincoln marched his troops out of Charleston. According to the terms of surrender, the American captives spent the rest of the war imprisoned on British prison ships in Charleston Harbor.

Massachusetts adopted a new constitution that stated, "all men are born free and equal," including black slaves.
- June 11, 1780

The Americans suffered a major defeat at the Battle of Camden in South Carolina on August 16, 1780. When the battle started, the Americans outnumbered the British two to one, but the weakened and sick American soldiers were unable to fight the British.

Two American Generals - Different choices

General Benedict Arnold was an American officer who conspired with the British to turn over West Point in September 1780. The plot failed and he became a British officer and led British troops against the Americans.

General Nathanael Greene was named the commander of the Southern Army in October 1780. He began a strategy to rally support and wear down the British military. He led them on a six-month chase through South Carolina, North Carolina and Virginia.

Battle at Kings Mountain Led to Final Victory

A volunteer force of 900 Overmountain Men defeated British Major Patrick Ferguson's 1,018 man loyalist regiment on a small mountain that straddles the North and South Carolina border on October 7, 1780. Their victory was the first link in a chain of events that ultimately led to the surrender of the British Army 12 months and 12 days later at Yorktown, Virginia.

The Overmountain Men became outraged when they received a message from British Major Ferguson. The message read: "If you do not desist your opposition to the British Arms, I shall march this army over the mountains, hang your leaders, and lay waste to your country with fire and sword."

Isaac Shelby and John Sevier, prominent militia leaders in the region, sent word for volunteers who wanted to confront Major Ferguson to meet at Sycamore Shoals in North Carolina on September 25. The frontiersmen came from the hills and valleys west of the Appalachian Mountains of North Carolina, Tennessee, Virginia, South Carolina and Georgia. On September 26, more than a thousand angry men started marching towards Kings Mountain. Most were on horseback, the rest walked.

After they arrived at Kings Mountain on October 7, they immediately surrounded the small mountain and began their Indian style assault – shooting from behind trees and rocks with their Kentucky and Pennsylvania long rifles. When the 65 minute battle ended, 157 of Ferguson's men were killed, 163 wounded and the remaining 698 were captured. The patriot losses included 28 killed, 62 wounded and none captured.

Major Ferguson was killed during the battle. He made an easy target for the Overmountain Men by riding his horse wearing a green and white checked duster-shirt over his uniform. He was buried on the battlefield.

It was an unexpected but satisfying victory that provided a giant leap in America's struggle for independence. Thomas Jefferson called the Kings Mountain victory, "the turn of the tide of success" in the War for Independence.

> "Let each one of you be your own officer, and do the very best you can, taking every care you can of yourselves, and availing yourselves of every advantage that chance may throw in your way. If in the woods, shelter yourselves, and give them Indian play; advance from tree to tree, pressing the enemy and killing and disabling all you can."
>
> - Isaac Shelby, Overmountain Leader

The World Turned Upside Down

1781

The French fleet defeated the British off the coast of Cape Henry, a short distance from Yorktown.

- **JANUARY 17** - AMERICAN ACTION: American regular army and militia led by General Daniel Morgan defeated Banastre Tarleton's loyalists forces at the Battle of Cowpens in South Carolina.
- **MARCH 15** - BRITISH ACTION: The British won the Battle of Guilford Courthouse in North Carolina after the Americans abandoned the battlefield.
- **MAY 22 to JUNE 18** - AMERICAN ACTION: The Continental Army led by Major General Nathanael Greene and "Light Horse" Harry Lee confronted British loyalists in a siege at Ninety-Six, South Carolina. The Americans withdrew on June 18.
- **JUNE 10** - AMERICAN ACTION: Americans and French joined forces in Virginia to oppose British troops under Benedict Arnold and General Cornwallis.
- **JUNE 11** - AMERICAN ACTION: Congress appointed a Peace Commission to join John Adams in his negotiations with the British.
- **AUGUST 1** - BRITISH ACTION: General Cornwallis and his 10,000 tired soldiers stopped to rest at the small port of Yorktown, Virginia.
- **AUGUST 14** - AMERICAN ACTION: General Washington abruptly changed plans and abandoned an attack on New York and instead marched to Yorktown.
- **AUGUST 30** - FRENCH ACTION: Admiral de Grasse's French fleet arrived off Yorktown, Virginia.
- **SEPTEMBER 5 to 8** - FRENCH ACTION: Off the Yorktown coast, a major naval battle between the French and British fleets resulted in a major victory for the French. The British fleet retreated to New York.
- **SEPTEMBER 14 to 24** - FRENCH ACTION: Admiral de Grasse sent his ships up the Chesapeake Bay to transport the armies of George Washington and General Jean-Baptiste Rochambeau to Yorktown.
- **SEPTEMBER 26** - AMERICAN ACTION: Washington and Rochambeau joined forces near Williamsburg to prepare for battle against the British.
- **SEPTEMBER 28** - AMERICAN ACTION: General Washington with a combined allied army of 17,000 men began the siege of Yorktown.
- **OCTOBER 17 and 18** - BRITISH ACTION: As Allied forces tightened the circle, the British sent out a flag of truce. AMERICAN, FRENCH & BRITISH ACTION: American, French and British officers negotiated terms of General Cornwallis' surrender.
- **OCTOBER 19** - BRITISH ACTION: The British band played "The World Turned Upside Down" while the Redcoats laid down their weapons and surrendered.

Battle of Cowpens
Morgan's Troop Deployment Won Decisive Victory

On January 17, American General Daniel Morgan defeated British Lieutenant-Colonel Banastre Tarleton's loyalist forces in a South Carolina pasture known as Hannah's Cowpens.

The Americans won a decisive victory with a new and unique deployment of troops. Morgan devised an effective way to use militia along with regular troops that maximized their combined strengths.

The British had 100 killed, 229 wounded and 829 captured. American casualties were light: 12 killed, 60 wounded and no captives.

The victories at Kings Mountain and Cowpens increased American morale and confidence and weakened the British. British defeats also convinced General Charles Cornwallis to pull his troops out of South Carolina and move to Virginia.

British Lieutenant-Colonel Banastre Tarleton became known in America as "the butcher" because of his brutal tactics and actions at the Battle of Waxhaws.

Details of Morgan's Bold Plan

Morgan's plan was to use the militia to make the Redcoats think the battle would be easy to win, then surprise them with a strong force that would lead to an American victory.

The night before Morgan instructed his 1,000 soldiers to fire two rounds, two well-placed shots, and then to orderly withdraw to the rear.

On the front line he stationed 150 mountaineer sharpshooters. The second and third lines were militia that were known to retreat soon after the Redcoats started firing. Morgan placed his main line on a hill. The rest were concealed on the back side of the hill.

After the first three lines fired their weapons two times and retreated, the Redcoats expected the final line to retreat, but they held fast. The Redcoats faced veteran Continental soldiers, 200 riflemen, 100 Continental dragoons, and hundreds of militia.

Morgan's plan was so successful that it became a pattern for other American officers.

Battle of Guilford Courthouse
British Victory Came at a Very High Price

Under General Charles Cornwallis' command, the British defeated the Americans at Guilford Courthouse after American General Nathanael Greene ordered his troops to retreat. The victory came at a cost of almost 25 percent of Cornwallis' army. More than 550 were killed, wounded or captured on March 15.

At one point during the battle, Cornwallis became so desperate that he ordered his cannons to be fired that were too close to his own lines, and a good number of his own men were killed and wounded.

Knowing they had dealt the British army a harsh blow, General Greene retreated to prevent more deaths and harm to his men. He wanted to save them for another day. American casualties totaled 78 killed and 183 wounded; records are not available on how many were captured.

Not only did the loss of so many soldiers weaken Cornwallis' army, but they were also low on supplies and would be unable to get new troops. He was a long way from Wilmington, North Carolina, where supplies and soldiers were available.

After the battle, Cornwallis began to move his army into Virginia. The Americans followed and harassed the British as they eventually marched to Yorktown, Virginia, where Cornwallis' army would surrender and end the war seven months later.

> *"Another such victory would ruin the British army."*
> – Charles James Fox, British Statesman

Tide of War Turned for the Americans

British troops had some success after moving the focus of the war to the southern colonies. However, beginning with the Battle of Kings Mountain everything changed. The decisive victory over British Major Patrick Ferguson's loyalist regiment on Kings Mountain, followed by Cowpens and Guilford Courthouse altered the course of the war in America's favor.

October 19 - British Surrendered at Yorktown

A combined force of 17,600 American and French troops began the siege of Yorktown on September 28. General Charles Cornwallis' 8,300 troops were trapped at Yorktown with their backs against the York River.

Following Washington's orders, the Marquis de Lafayette blocked Cornwallis' escape by land while the French fleet, under the command of Admiral de Grasse, blocked an escape by sea.

Over time, the American and French troops built two trenches that encircled the British army.

> *"Against so powerful an attack, we cannot hope to make a very long resistance."*
>
> *- General Charles Cornwallis*

American General Benjamin Lincoln, mounted on a white horse in the center, extended his right hand to receive General Cornwallis' sword from General Charles O'Hara. George Washington is pictured to the right of Lincoln on a brown horse.

The allied forces bombarded the Redcoats – day and night – with cannons, howitzers and mortars. The Americans and French were relentless in their efforts to defeat the British.

General Cornwallis soon realized that surrender was their only option.

On October 17, a British officer and drummer were seen standing on one of the redoubts waving a white flag. The officer carried a note from General Cornwallis to General Washington requesting a cease fire. The next day an American and a French officer met with two British officers at Moore House to arrange surrender terms.

At 2 p.m. on October 19, approximately 7,000 British soldiers marched in single file between the American and French armies – a distance of more than a mile – and surrendered their weapons.

General Cornwallis claimed to be sick and did not attend the surrender ceremony. His second in command, General Charles O'Hara, presented Cornwallis' sword, according to military custom, to the American and French commanders.

The Siege of Yorktown was the last major battle of the American War for Independence.

> *"We waited with anxiety the termination of the armistice and as the time drew nearer our anxiety increased. The time at length arrived - it passed, and all remained quiet. And now we concluded that we had obtained what we had taken so much pains for, for which we had encountered so many dangers, and had so anxiously wished. Before night we were informed that the British had surrendered and that the siege was ended."*
>
> *- Diary of Joseph Plumb Martin Continental Soldier*

Washington: A Fearless Commander-in-Chief

General Washington was never wounded during his long years of leading the Continental Army. Dressed in his colorful general's uniform and standing 6 feet 3 inches tall, he made a distinctive and easy target for Redcoats and Hessians. He and his staff often found holes in his cloak and hat, but he never suffered a wound.

Most generals stayed safely behind the battle where they used messengers and drummers to convey instructions to field commanders. But not Washington. He fearlessly led from the front.

Thomas Jefferson once wrote: "He was incapable of fear, meeting personal dangers with the calmest unconcern."

> George Washington's Continental Army, with the help of volunteer militias, lost more battles than they won. Yet, they defeated the strongest, the best organized and the best equipped army on earth.

Washington's Two War Horses

George Washington rode two horses during the American Revolution – Nelson and Blueskin. He preferred Nelson because he was a calm horse. Cannon fire and the startling sounds of battle did not effect him. Nelson was a tall chestnut with a white blaze on his face and two white feet. He was 15-years old when Washington received him as a gift from fellow Virginian Thomas Nelson.

Blueskin is the horse we most often see in Washington's war portraits. He was a gray stallion with Arabian heritage. Colonel Benjamin Tasker Dulany of Maryland gave the horse to Washington.

Both horses retired to Mount Vernon after the war. Nelson lived to the age of 27. History does not record how old Blueskin was when he died.

Blueskin

Nelson

Moving Towards Peace

1782

- **FEBRUARY 27** - BRITISH ACTION: The House of Commons voted to stop the war.
- **MARCH 5** - BRITISH ACTION: Parliament empowered the King to negotiate peace with the United States.
- **MARCH 20** - BRITISH ACTION: British Prime Minister Lord North resigned. He was succeeded by Lord Rockingham who sought immediate negotiations with the Americans.
- **APRIL 4** - BRITISH ACTION: Sir Guy Carleton became the new commander of British forces in America, replacing General William Clinton. He implemented a new policy to end hostilities and send British troops back to England.
- **APRIL 12** - AMERICAN & BRITISH ACTION: Peace talks began in Paris between Benjamin Franklin and Richard Oswald of Britain.
- **JUNE 20** - AMERICAN ACTION: Congress adopted the Great Seal of the United States of America and designated the bald eagle as the national bird.
- **NOVEMBER 30** - AMERICAN & BRITISH ACTION: A preliminary peace treaty was signed in Paris. Terms included recognition of American independence; boundaries of the United States were established; and all British forces would withdraw from America.
- **DECEMBER 14** - BRITISH ACTION: British forces evacuated Charleston, South Carolina.

British Evacuated Charleston Before Christmas

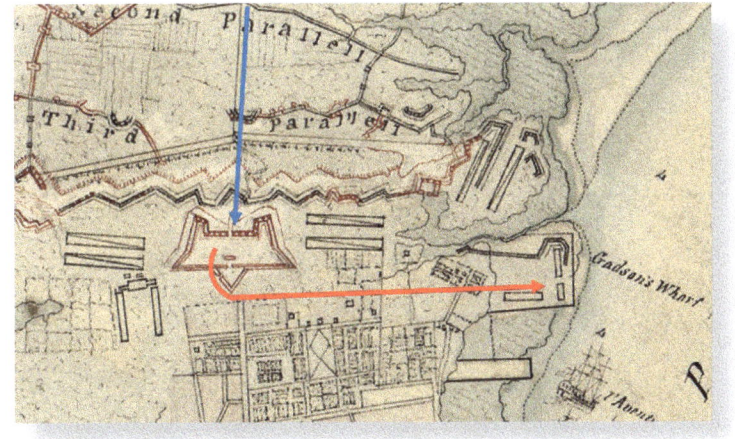

The red line represents the path of the British troops retreating from the town gates on December 14, 1782. The blue line represents the Americans advancing down King Street. Detail from map reads: "The Investiture of Charleston by the English" from the Library of Congress.

June 20, 1782
Congress Adopted the Great Seal of the United States

Preliminary sketch of the Great Seal

Victorious Continental Army Disbanded
1783

- **FEBRUARY 3** - INTERNATIONAL ACTION: Spain, Sweden, Denmark and Russia formally recognized the United States of America as an independent country.
- **FEBRUARY 4** - BRITISH ACTION: The British government officially declared an end to hostilities in America.
- **APRIL 11** - AMERICAN ACTION: Congress officially declared an end to the Revolutionary War.
- **APRIL 15** - AMERICAN ACTION: Congress ratified the preliminary peace treaty with Great Britain.
- **JUNE 13** - AMERICAN ACTION: The main body of the Continental Army was disbanded.
- **SEPTEMBER 3** - AMERICAN & BRITISH ACTION: The Treaty of Paris was signed by representative of the United States and Great Britain.
- **NOVEMBER 2** - AMERICAN ACTION: George Washington delivered his farewell address to his military officers at Fraunces Tavern in New York City.
- **NOVEMBER 3** - AMERICAN ACTION: The remaining American troops were discharged.
- **NOVEMBER 25** - AMERICAN ACTION: Three months after the peace treaty had been signed, the last British soldiers departed New York for England.

Farewell to the Army

General Washington delivered his farewell orders to the Continental Army on November 2. He declared his officers and men to be "one patriotic band of Brothers" for their valiant and noble sacrifices, conduct and victorious efforts during the war for independence.

General Washington and the Continental Army triumphantly entered New York City on November 25, seven years after the British army established martial law. They entered the city as the last Redcoats were boarding ships for England.

Treaty of Paris...

◆ Acknowledged Independent & Sovereign United States of America
◆ Established Territorial Boundaries ◆ Freed Prisoners of War

1781

JUNE 11 - The Continental Congress named five peace commissioners to negotiate with British representatives – John Adams, Benjamin Franklin, John Jay, Thomas Jefferson and Henry Laurens.

JUNE 15 - The Continental Congress instructed the peace commissioners "to negotiate a treaty of peace on behalf of the United States. . . .You are to accede to no Treaty of Peace which shall not be such as may first effectually secure the Independence and Sovereignty of the 13 United States. . . . You are therefore at liberty to secure the Interest of the United States in such manner as Circumstances may direct."

Unfinished portrait of American peace commissioners: John Jay, John Adams, Benjamin Franklin and Henry Laurens. The man behind Franklin is his grandson. Painted by Benjamin West.

Treaty's last page with peace commissioners' signatures.

1782

MARCH 5 - Parliament authorized peace negotiations.
APRIL 12 - Peace talks began in Paris.
NOVEMBER 30 - American and British peace commissioners signed the preliminary Treaty of Paris.

1783

JANUARY 20 - American, British, French and Spanish representatives signed a provisional peace treaty proclaiming an end to hostilities.
FEBRUARY 4 - England officially declared an end to hostilities.
APRIL 11 - Congress officially declared an end to the war.
SEPTEMBER 3 - The official Treaty of Paris was signed by John Adams, John Jay, Benjamin Franklin and David Hartley and was immediately dispatched to Congress and King George III for ratification.

1784

JANUARY 14 - Congress voted to approve the Treaty of Paris.
APRIL 9 - King George III ratified the treaty five weeks after the deadline.

Bibliography

In addition to more than 40 years of reading, research and study about the American Revolution, the Declaration of Independence and Thomas Jefferson, I would like to acknowledge the following resources:

American Battlefield Trust, battlefields.org
American History Central, americanhistorycentral.com
American Revolutionary War Facts, american-revolutionary-war-facts.com
British Battles, britishbattles.com
Colonial Williamsburg, history.org
Encyclopedia Britannica, britannica.com
George Washington's Mount Vernon, mountvernon.org
History Central, historycentral.com
Jefferson's Monticello, home.monticello.org
John Adams Historical Society, john-adams-heritage.com
Journal of the American Revolution, allthingsliberty.com
Massachusetts Historical Society, masshist.org
National Park Service, nps.gov/revwar
National Archives, archives.gov
Revolutionary War and Beyond, revolutionary-war-and-beyond.com
Revolutionary-War.net, Revolutionary-War.net
RevolutionaryWarArchives, revolutionarywararchives.org
The American Revolution, theamericanrevolution.org
The American Revolutionary War, revolutionary-war.net
The History Place, historyplace.com
The Library of Congress, loc.gov
U.S. History, ushistory.org

Image Credits

COVER
1-Tax on Tea cartoon, newsela.com/read/lib-ushistory-townshend-acts. 2-Battle of Guilford Courthouse Militia by Don Troiani, National Park Service Museum. 3-Boston Massacre engraving by Paul Revere, Wikimedia. 4-Benjamin Franklin's Join or Die cartoon, Benjamin Franklin Tercentenary, benfranklin300.org. 5-The Sentry by Andrew Knez, Jr., andrewknezjr.com. 6-The Tocsin of Liberty by Currier & Ives, Library of Congress. 7-Committee of Five, Founding Fathers: The Declaration Committee, by John Buxton, Bill of Rights Institute. 8-Surrender at Yorktown (Detail) by John Trumbull, britishbattles.com. 9-Dennis Parker's Photo, copyright owned by author.

TABLE OF CONTENTS
Spirit of 76 by Archibald MacNeal Willard, Wikimedia.

PAGE 2
Stand Your Ground, Lexington Common by Don Troiani, National Guard Heritage, Department of the Army.

PAGE 3
Protesting the Stamp Act in Boston 1765, engraving by Daniel Chodowiecki, Library of Congress.

PAGE 4
Battle of Quebec by Richard Caton Woodville, Tate Institute, National Collection of British Art, britishbattles.com.

PAGE 5
1-The Royal Proclamation of 1763, Library and Archives of Canada. 2-Proclamation Map, adapted from National Atlas of the United States. 3-Daniel Boone Leading the Settlers Through the Cumberland Gap by David Wright, Cumberland Gap Historical National Park.

PAGE 6
1-Original 13 British Colonies map, SDPB Educational Programing, sdpb.org 2-Benjamin Franklin's Join or Die cartoon, Benjamin Franklin Tercentenary, benfranklin300.org.

PAGE 7
The Rights of the British Colonies Asserted and Proved, Museum Collections, Valley Forge National Historical Park (VAFO 63957), nps.gov.

PAGE 8
1-Three-pence note, printed by Benjamin Franklin and David Hall, Wikimedia. 2-Bostonians Reading the Stamp Act, New York Public Library Digital Collection.

PAGE 9
Patrick Henry addressing Virginia Assembly, engraving by Henry Bryan Hall after a painting by Alonzo Chappel, New York Public Library.

PAGE 10
1-Quartering Act graphic by Beverly Parker, type on 18th century kitchen, public domain image. 2-Patrick Henry by George Bagby Matthews, Wikimedia.

PAGE 11
1-No Taxation graphic by Beverly Parker, British Flag, wallpaper-house.com 2-Sons of Liberty Notice, Massachusetts Historical Society.

PAGE 12
British Parliament, The House of Commons 1793-94 by Karl Anton Hickel, National Portrait Gallery, npg.org.uk.

PAGE 13
1-Coat of Arms of the British East India Company, Wikimedia. 2-Townshend Acts parchment graphic by Dennis Parker. 3-Tax on Tea cartoon, newsela.com/read/lib-ushistory-townshend-acts.

PAGE 14
Sam Adams' Signature, Wikimedia, adapted by Beverly Parker.

PAGE 15
1-Samuel Adams by John Singleton Copley, Wikiart. 2- Redcoats in Boston, posted by Mark Beerdom, American War Museum.

Image Credits - Continued

PAGE 16
Raleigh Tavern drawing by Shirley Fout Miller, 1988 Colonial Williamsburg Calendar.

PAGE 17
Boston Massacre engraving by Paul Revere, Wikimedia.

PAGE 18
Battle of Alamance 1771, illustration for cover of the Commemorative Souvenir Program, Battle of Alamance Bicentennial, 1971.

PAGE 19
Destruction of the *Gaspée* by W.C. Jackson, *Blue Jackets of 1776*, published 1888.

PAGE 20
Committee for Tar and Feathering Notice, Wikimedia.

PAGE 21
1-Boston Tea Party, engraving, Encyclopaedia Britannica. 2-Boston Tea Ship image, Blogspot of J.L. Bell, boston1775.blogspot.com.

PAGE 22
Coat of Arms of Great Britain 1714-1801, Wikimedia.

PAGE 23
1-Petition of 1774, Massachusetts Historical Society. 2-First Continental Congress 1774 by Allyn Cox, U.S. Capitol mural.

PAGE 24
Paul Revere's Ride by N.C. Wyeth, Tes.com/uk.

PAGE 25
1-Battle on Lexington Green, April 1775 by William Barnes Wollen, britishbattles.com. 2-Battle of Concord, April 1775 by Charles Henry Granger, britishbattles.com.

PAGE 26
The Battle of Lexington, April 19th, 1775, etched by Amos Doolittle, printer's ink and watercolor, Connecticut Historical Society.

PAGE 27
Assembly Room, Independence Hall, Philadelphia, Wikimedia.

PAGE 28
George Washington, first commander, painting, U.S. Army Center of Military History, photo by Bill Rosenburg, army.mil.

PAGE 29
1-Battle of Bunker Hill by Don Troiani, pritzkermilitary.org. 2-Watching the Fight at Bunker Hill by Howard Pyle, sonofthesouth.net.

PAGE 30
1-Olive Branch, free clip art, Google images. 2-Olive Branch Petition, digitalcollections.nypl.org.

PAGE 31
1-U.S. Naval Jack flag, Wikimedia. 2-View of Boston Harbor by Franz Xaver Habermann 1770, Library of Congress.

PAGE 32
1-General George Washington by Charles Peale Polk, circa 1790, Virginia Museum of History and Culture. 2-General Thomas Gage by John Singleton Copley, Yale Center for British Art, Wikimedia. 3-General William Howe by Charles Corbutt, Brown University, dl.lib.brown.edu. 4-General Henry Clinton by Andrea Soldi, The American Museum in Britain, americanmuseum.org.

PAGE 33
1-2nd New Jersey Regiment Private 1776 by Don Troiani, groundreport.com. 2-British Line Infantryman, early Revolutionary War by Don Troiani, mzayat.com.

PAGE 34
Minutemen of the Revolution by Currier & Ives, Library of Congress.

PAGE 35
African American Slaves in Revolutionary War, buildnationblog.wordpress.com.

PAGE 36
1-Continental Infantry Equipment, FlintlockandTomahawk.blogspot.com. 2-Revolutionary Long Rifle, Wikimedia. 3-Kentucky Long Rifle, Wikimedia.

PAGE 37
1-Flintlock Rifle Loading Guide, survivalistboards.com. 2-Charleville Musket, Wikimedia. 3-Brown Bess Musket, Wikimedia.

PAGE 39
1-*Common Sense*, pamphlet cover, Google education site. 2-Thomas Paine by Auguste Milliére, Wikimedia. 3-Long Island Battle by Charles Henry Granger, britishbattles.com.

PAGE 40
1-Halifax Resolves mural by Francis Vandeveer Kughler, UNC School of Government. 2-Halifax Resolves, North Carolina in the Revolution by Joshua Simmons, middle school teacher, slideshare.net.

PAGE 41
Lee Resolution, Wikimedia.

PAGE 42
1-Committee of Five, Founding Fathers: The Declaration Committee by John Buxton, Bill of Rights Institute.

PAGE 43
1-Graff House illustration by Robert Shaw, circa 1906, Library of Congress. 2-Graff House Parlor, National Park Service. 3-Portable Desk, Library of Congress. 4-Silver Pen, Library of Congress. 5-Declaration rough draft, (Detail) "Citizens Not Subjects", Library of Congress.

PAGE 44
1-Jefferson's original Declaration rough draft, Library of Congress. 2-Caesar Rodney's Ride, graphic by Beverly Parker.

PAGE 46
Declaration of Independence, Library of Congress.

PAGE 47
1-King George's Diary on July 4th, graphic by Dennis Parker. 2-18th Century Press, Charles Mills mural, Benjamin Franklin Historical Society.

PAGE 48
1-Brown Bess Musket, Wikimedia. 2-Revolutionary War drum, Museum of the American Revolution.

PAGE 49
1-Signing of the Declaration of Independence by H.A. Ogden, Public Domain 2-Quill Pen, free clip art, gallery.yopriceville.com.

Image Credits - Continued

PAGE 50
1-Thomas Jefferson by Charles Wilson Peale, Library of Congress. 2-Jack Jouett Ride, graphic by Beverly Parker.
PAGE 51
King George III by Johann Zoffany, Wikimedia.
PAGE 52
1-Hessian-Cassell Leib Infantry Grenadier 1776-1784 by Keith Rocco, pinterest.co.uk. 2-Battle of Trenton by Charles McBarron, Wikimedia.
PAGE 53
1-Grand Union Flag, Wikimedia. 2-Betsy Ross Flag, Wikimedia.
PAGE 54
1-First Meeting of Washington and Lafayette, Currier & Ives, metmuseum.org, public domain. 2-Lafayette Coat of Arms, Wikimedia.
PAGE 55
1-"Nation Makers" - Battle of Brandywine Creek by Howard Pyle, brandywinemuseum.org, Wikimedia. 2-Major Patrick Ferguson by Thomas Kelly Pauley, knowitall.org.
PAGE 56
Burgoyne's Surrender at Saratoga by Percy Moran, Library of Congress.
PAGE 57
1-Articles of Confederation cartoon, resourcesforhistoryteachers.wikispaces.com. 2-Winter at Valley Forge 1778, emergingrevolutionarywar.org.
PAGE 58
1-Washington's Camp Marquee, Museum of the American Revolution. 2-Washington's Headquarters Flag, Museum of the American Revolution. 3-Washington's Note to General Howe, Library of Congress.
PAGE 59
Royal Standard of the King of France 1778. Wikimedia.
PAGE 60
Von Steuben Drilling American Recruits at Valley Forge 1778 by Steve Noon, posted by Mark Beerdom.

PAGE 62
1-Battle of Camden by Pamela Patrick White 2008, Delaware Public Archives, Delaware Sons of the American Revolution. 2-Benedict Arnold by Thomas Hart, Wikimedia. 3-Nathanael Greene by James Ward, Greene County Government, Pennsylvania.
PAGE 63
The Patriot Victory at Kings Mountain, by artist Richard Luce, Kings Mountain National Military Park.
PAGE 64
Battle of the Virginia Capes by V. Zveg, Wikimedia.
PAGE 65
The Battle of Cowpens by H. Charles McBarron, Cowpens National Battlefield, National Park Service.
PAGE 66
Battle of Guilford Courthouse by H. Charles McBarron, Wikimedia.
PAGE 67
Surrender at Yorktown by John Trumbull, britishbattles.com.
PAGE 68
1-George Washington and Blueskin by Rembrandt Peale, drbenjaminchurchjr.blogspot.com. 2-George Washington and Nelson, chrisstevensonauthor.com.
PAGE 69
1-British Evacuate Charleston map, Charleston County Public Library. 2-Preliminary sketch of the Great Seal of the United States, Wikimedia.
PAGE 70
Washington's Entry to New York (Detail) by Edmund P. Restein, Library of Congress.
PAGE 71
1-Unfinished Portrait of American Peace Commissioners by Benjamin West, Wikimedia. 2-Signed Treaty of Paris 1783, Wikimedia.